THE CHILDANDARIANS

SERBIAN MONKS
ON THE GREEN MOUNTAIN

BY SLAVKO P. TODOROVICH

EAST EUROPEAN MONOGRAPHS, BOULDER
DISTRIBUTED BY COLUMBIA UNIVERSITY PRESS, NEW YORK

1989

EAST EUROPEAN MONOGRAPHS, NO. CCLXIV

TABLE OF CONTENTS

ACKNOWLEDGMENTS

In the preparation of this manuscript I became indebted to many people. The scope of this indebtedness cannot be expressed fully in this acknowledgment. A great many acquaintances and friends came to my rescue while I was struggling to put together a story that I believed was interesting and significant. I imposed upon their good will, their expertise, their precious time, and their unlimited patience.

I remain deeply indebted to these humble and self-effacing Mount Athos monks who refrained from any sign of resentment toward an outsider who kept returning and disturbing their peace. I still cannot get over the hospitality and the generosity of Chilandar Monastery monks who welcomed my prolonged visits and opened not only their archives and treasures but their hearts as well.

Special acknowledgment is due to Father Mitrofan who patiently answered all my letters and constant queries; to Father Vasilije who spent many evenings in conversation with me; and in particular to Pro-Hegumen Nikanor, whose astuteness and sagacity, good humor and cordiality seems to win over every visitor.

I cannot adequately express the scope of my appreciation and dependence upon the advice and guidance of Dr. Alex N. Dragnich (Professor Emeritus, ii Vanderbilt University) who helped me in many ways. I also had the good fortune of being the recipient of initial encouragement and support of Dr. Mirjana Zivojinovic of the Byzantology Institute of the Serbian Academy of Sciences and Arts (Belgrade) during her fellowship year in the United States.

It gives me great pleasure to express my gratitude to personal friends: Dr. Carl A. Baer, Mary Shepherdson, and Lucy Rosenberg all of whom set aside time and energy to read parts of the manuscript and to offer valuable suggestions. My thanks go to Angie Mamula who typed the first

FOREWARD

This is the story about the special breed of Serbian monks living on Mount Athos in Greece who, by the grace of God and out of national necessity, year after year had to deal with secular affairs of their homeland, Serbia. For eight long centuries, the history of Serbia and the history of the Chilandar* Monastery were tightly webbed. In this context, the term "Chilandarians" acquired special significance not only in the spiritual history of the Serbian nation, but in the political realm as well.

Chilandar Monastery was built by the Grand Zhupan Nemanya (1166-1196), the founding father of Medieval Serbia. Turning to monasticism in his old age, Nemanya went to Mount Athos with one express wish in mind — to build a Serbian monastery in the center of Eastern (Byzantine) Orthodoxy. He also looked forward to being with his youngest son Sava (later Saint Sava) already a monk on Athos.

The aging father and his youthful son made sure the monastery was built by special authorization of the Byzantine Emperor (Alexios III Angelos, 1195-1203), who gave the site on Mount Athos in "perpetuity to the Serbs." The Emperor's special edict to this effect guaranteed that in the future Chilandar would have the high rank of an "imperial monastery."

Frail and of old age, Nemanya did not live long in his monastery. Yet he was there long enough to instill in the monks a sense of duty and moral obligation to their homeland. On his deathbed Nemanya was a happy man: he had brought Serbia into the family of nations, and he had put the Serbian monastery on the map of the Holy Mountain. Last but not least, he had found his fugitive son Sava, with whom he had always shared the inner call to serve God.

*Although the Serbs spell it Hilandar, I have chosen the spelling used by most Byzantine scholars.

Nemanya's spiritual children, the Chilandarians, never forgot the guidance they received during Nemanya's brief but powerfull presence in the monastery. They pledged to follow in the footsteps of their spiritual father, and never to forsake allegiance to their native land. In awesome veneration and deep respect, they realized that Chilandar monastery and their homeland, Serbia, were of one parent.

The loyalty of Chilandarians to their mentor Nemanya and to their native land, both in times of glory and in periods of defeat, remained infinite and unbounded. In the Middle Ages, Chilandar provided the nation with teachers and missionaries, priests, abbots and high ecclesiastics, liturgy books and scriptures. This was only a part of what Chilandar contributed to the forming of Serbian statehood. Generations of Chilandar theologians, devoted scribes, and talented authors added to the literary fund of the nation. At the same time, skillful mediators, cunning diplomats, and statecraft experts among them were fully involved in church and state affairs. Chilandar Monastery seem to have had a bottomless bag of men of all seasons and abilities ready to serve the nation.

In Medieval Serbia one meets Chilandarians everywhere. They are the confidants of royal heads, confessors of monarchs and their families, members of state assemblies and councils, heads of official delegations, trusted messengers commuting between the capitals of Serbia and Byzantium or serving as special envoys in foreign chanceries. These Serbian monks, who entered the monastery in order to seek communion with the Deity and the heavens, never abandoned Serbia's earthly concerns.

For eight centuries Chilandarians stood ready to answer the nation's call, just as Nemanya would have done. On more than one occasion, the task was formidable and out of the ordinary. It took a Chilandarian to face the aggressive Pontiff of Rome and to make him blink. Similarly, it took a Chilandarian to talk the Ecumenical Patriarch into relenting his grip on the Serbian Orthodox Church.

Whenever the nation was in need of an astute connoisseur of Greek ways and of the pitfalls of the Byzantine political maze, inevitably the choice would fall upon a seasoned veteran from Chilandar. It was a Chilandarian who journeyed to Moscow to remind Ivan the Terrible of his obligation to aid enslaved Slavs and their monasteries under Turkish rule. It is noteworthy that Chilandarians endured admirably during the Turkish period, constantly bringing solace and giving comfort to their compatriots. "White Chilandar" loomed large on a distant horizon in those trying times.

In the 19th century, when the long expected liberation of Serbia finally occurred, the nation rushed to her monastery, there to find the elsewhere downtrodden and tyrannized heritage intact and preserved. Hundreds of manuscripts and documents, written in Old Serbian and in Greek, and hidden from the evil eye of the occupier, waited to be discovered by the freed nation.

Today, hosts of Serbian pilgrims come to visit the monastery custodians and to talk to the Chilandarians. Restricted to short time stays, the visitors hurry to express admiration and gratitude. The monks, for their part, are not distracted from their monastic routine, which consist of "day and night reverence of the name of God." At the same time, they cannot but note with satisfaction the revival of traditional values among the Serbs. The Chilandarians find it equally comforting to observe the increased interest of scholars in the cultural wealth of the monastery. This is in keeping with the past, for never was a Chilandarian one to turn a deaf ear to a learned person or a man of letters.

In lieu of an Introduction

In Northern Greece, projecting into the Aegean Sea from Macedonia, there is a mountainous peninsula called Khalkidiki (Chalcidice). Aristotle died there; St. Paul arduously trekked over it to address the Thessalonians; and the famous Roman trade route (Via Egnatia) was a difficult passageway over its grounds.

At the terminus of the peninsula are three lengthy promontories. Seen from above, the strangely shaped land resembles the hand of a giant; the three fingers appear as though reaching for an object deep in water. These jutted extensions are known as Kassandra (in the West), Sithonia (in the center), and Mount Athos (in the East). The latter is named after its massive rock, which appears to be soaring into the clouds, at the end of the promontory. However, the Greeks have thought of another name for this protracted stretch of land, a name more fitting to their popular concept of the promontory. They call it Aghion Oros (The Holy Mountain). "Holy"— because holy men live there. Ever since the third century, these rock-ribbed lanscapes have served as a retreat for anchorites and ascetics.

As an exclusive realm of men who pay honor to the Deity, the Holy Mountain always attracted Byzantine, Greek, and Slav Christians of the Eastern Rite. In the early days, many of those who were persecuted by Arab invaders and iconoclasts moved to the Holy Mountain. The promontory offered ideal seclusion to those retreating from the secular world, to those seeking evasion from despotic bishops, as well as to those who looked for a quiet place to meditate. Byzantine emperors and Turkish sultans, as well as latter day Greek monarchs, treated these religious men with courtesy and respect. By the 10th century, with the beginning of the era of tall monasteries, men of arts and letters arrived. The monasteries and their rich libraries attracted religious doctrinaires and scholars, as well as famous artists who came to decorate the walls and paint the icons. Their work is still there, miraculously clinging to crumbling mortar and worm-eaten wood.

An emperor's confessor, Ossios Athanasios, built the oldest of the Holy Mountain monasteries in existence today (Meghisti Lavra, 10th Century). At one time, the Holy Mountain had more than 40 monasteries, the population of which exceeded 40,000. Aghion Oros was considered the stronghold of Eastern Orthodoxy.

Byzantine emperors vied with one another in lavishly bestowing Mount Athos monasteries with endowments. Patronage over a Holy Mountain monastery positively added to the reputation and status of the endower. This custom was soon to be emulated by rulers of even the smallest nations seeking recognition, Nemanya, the founder of Serbia and the progenitor of the Nemanjic dynasty, was one of those rulers. In 1198, on the Holy Mountain (the spiritual center of Byzantium) Nemanya built the Serbian monastery Chilandar (Hilandar). He seemed to have realized, even if belatedly, that winning the confidence of the Mount Athos monks was more effective than rebellion and political intrigues. Good standing in Karyes, the capital of Mount Athos, was essential for acceptance in Constantinople, the capital of Byzantium.

By the time Nemanya went to Mount Athos, his charismatic son had already won the esteem of many abbots and monastery elders there, as well as a certain influence at the office of the Primus (Protos). Also, the retired old statesman, Nemanya, did not lack experience in either government or ecclesiastical affairs. He had no difficulty in winning the Protos over to his side, and obtaining permission to build his own monastery on the Holy Mountain. Chances were that, once the Protos agreed, neither the emperor nor the patriarch in Constantinople would deny the petitioner.

The monastery was still being built when the aged Nemanya took leave from this world. He died in Chilandar peacefully, confident and certain that his nation had definitely been recognized in Constantinople, and that there was a future for his newly-founded state. Now it was up to the monks, the Chilandarians, to continue with the original plans of Nemanya. Serving God and nation, Chilandarians tenaciously persevered through thick and thin for eight centuries.

In the Middle Ages, Chilandarians endowed Serbia with illustrious ecclesiastics, eminent authors, and talented diplomats. Throughout the seemingly endless period of Turkish domination, as the homeland was put to the sword of Islam, Chilandarians kept the flame of hope from being extinguished. For five centuries they acted as custodians of the national heritage. In the 19th century, as the liberation of Serbia took place, Chilandarians provided the renascent nation — in search of a buried past — with rich repositories of historical and cultural records. The nation walked into its own treasure house — the Chilandar collections had preserved the nation's cultural identity.

In the spiritual life of the nation, Chilandarians continue to play an important role even today. The historical and cultural wealth of the monastery's library attracts Serbian scholars with various interests. A score of books and other publications have already been produced as a result of scholarly research. No doubt many more volumes will be published once the vast amount of stored material is organized methodically.

Today, Serbian laymen come to greet those who saved their roots and to admire the Serbian House of Worship on this sacred Eastern Orthodox soil. Once on the Greek Holy Mountain, Serbian visitors want only the Chilandarians to be their spiritual guides. They perceive the Chilandar Monastery as their font, their cradle, or the fold to which they feel the need to return, especially those who are still in a dazed state after a period of experimentation with lopsided Yugoslavism and dispirited Communism.

It seems that it all begins at the gate of the monastery when the Chilandarian monk greets the tired wayfarer with the words:

"Welcome brethren! . . . Welcome H O M E!"

Chapter I

THE HOLY MOUNTAIN
(Mount Athos)

Mountains since time immemorial, have drawn man to them for religious expression. Whether it be Olympus (Greece), Haleakala (Hawaii), Fuji - Sun (Japan), or Tabor and Sinai (Israel), it seeems that mountains made man feel closer to God. Mount Athos has done this for those who embraced and practiced Eastern Orthodoxy. For a variety of reasons this particular Mountain has offered comfort to many a searching soul. It is a gentle and beautiful mountain. Moreover, it has that degree of mystique and eeriness to suggest the supernatural. The ribbed landscape of rocks and the lush vegetation make it an ideal place for total isolation. Also, Mount Athos has two items a hermit needs: plenty of fresh water and an abundance of fruit. The climate is ideal — the searing sun and the soaking rains make a perfect balance. There is an abundance of sea food, and the olive groves supply the cooking oil. Last but not least, the monastery cellars are guaranteed tons of good wine-making grapes.

The landscape of Athos resembles a giant sculptured garden. Its rocks reach skyward from deep-green bases, while dry river beds or ravines hide in impenetrable umbrage. Hillsides are covered with the scented growth of wild roses, myrtle, laurel and juniper. Monasteries are generally surrounded by thickets of oleanders, while citrus trees thrive inside their yards. Open meadows are famous for their wealth of pharmaceutical herbs, and no monastery would be caught without an herbalist. Adding a special touch to the landscape are the impressively erect cypress trees, resembling a pipe organ when clustered against the backdrop of steep mountainsides.

Mount Athos began as a haven and has remained one. Historically a refuge and a sanctuary, it gradually became the center of Eastern

Orthodoxy. In a sense, the 6,600 foot-high granite at the tip of the promontory is the spiritual lighthouse, illuminating the road to salvation.

Among the first to envision the mountain in such terms must have been the Monk Athanasios, friend and confessor of the famous 10th century Greek general, Nikephoros Phokas, known as "The Scourge of the Saracens." The two of them, while campaigning against the nomads in Asia Minor, decided to build a splendid monastery on Mount Athos and there to retire once the senseless killing ceased. Spoils and booty being abundant, the general provided the funding, while Athanasios took it upon himself to build the edifice.

The two friends ran into unforeseen difficulties. The hermits already living on Mount Athos rebelled against the prospect of living in the shadow of a grandiose establishment. They did not want a monastery to overpower their haven of huts. Their opposition, however, was doomed from the outset because Athanasios was supported by his influential friend Nikephoros, who in the meantime had been proclaimed Emperor of Byzantium (963 -969).

The Lavra of Saint Athanasios the holiest and the oldest of today's 20 monasteries of the Holy Mountain was the first battle the hermits lost. Soon after other giants, such as the Monasteries Vatopediou and Iveron, would dot the eremitical landscape. The hermits had at least one satisfaction. Neither of the two "oppressors" lived to enjoy their planned retirement. Nikephoros, the provider of funds, was killed in Constantinople by his wife and her lover. While Athanasios, the builder, died when the dome under construction came down on his head.

Such reversals, however, could not halt history. Neither could the hermits, who hurriedly elected a delegation to take their case directly to the new Emperor, John Tsimiskes (969-976). They depicted Athanasios as "an oppressor of the Mountain . . . who erected towers, changed the course of streams and brought pairs of oxen . . . planted vineyards and cultivated fields."

Tsimiskes listened but did not seem to hear the hermits. In the year 972, Mount Athos got its first TYPIKON (constitution) written on kidskin and subsequently referred to as "Tragos" (Billy goat). This signalled a definite victory for the monasteries over the hermits' huts. Ever since, the Great Lavra (Meghisti Lavra) of Athanasios has remained as the top-ranking monastery of the Holy Mountain. Bowing to powerful oppressors however did not mean the end of the hermits. The eremitical concept never died on the Mountain. Throughout history hermits coexisted with the monasteries, and many of them were later acclaimed as saints.

Those who chose to live in isolation and to persevere in utmost austerity, chronic fasting, and lifetime silence were viewed in awe by monks, venerated and held as examples of true faith. No monk living within the walls of the monastery ever forgot his brother in a mountain cave. No monk would allow himself to forget St. Peter the Athonite, who spent five decades in solitude and silence, living in a cave near the Great Lavra; or Saint Euthymios, who, annoyed by throngs of admiring monks, climbed a pillar-like rock and stayed there, slowly devoured by worms and vermin, until he fell to his death; or Saint Makarios, who once squashed a thirsty mosquito and lived in a swamp, naked ever after.

Legends of this kind sound strange, questionable, outlandish, and bizarre, yet they shape the thinking and ignite the imagination of the Holy Mountain monks. The history of the Mountain is replete with tales of this type, legends and symbolism. Amoung numerous allegories and expressions of religious principles none is stronger than the general belief in the omnipresence of the Mother of God and Her dominance over athonite matters.

The Virgin Mary, so the story goes, arrived at the Holy Mountain in the year 49 A.D., having sailed from Jerusalem with the intention of visiting Lazarus, at that time the Bishop of Cyprus. One of the Evangelists accompanied the Virgin Mary, but the monks are divided on who it was — Luke or Mark. Suddenly, the skies darkened, the sea whitecaps crested and a pea-soup fog covered the horizon. In the storm the navigator lost his course. As the weather cleared, the small boat was drifting along the beautiful but unknown coast. Sailors decided to anchor in a peaceful bay, close to where the Monastery Iveron stands today. The crew was told that the name of the little settlement was Dion (Klementos). As the Virgin Mary stepped ashore, the ground shook and all pagan statues and idols shattered to pieces. Watching the breathtaking landscape, the Virgin exclaimed: "This mountain is holy ground. Let it be my garden. Here let me remain."[1] Ever since, Our Lady, All Holy, The Mother of God, Theotokos, rules on the Holy Mountain! And nobody calls this land by any other name but "The Garden of Panaghia (Most Holy)." The term "garden" is in fact used in the sense of paradise, the garden of Eden, and the monks are often referred to as "black angels."

Serbian sources in describing the Holy Mountain, often called it " the earthly Garden of Eden," in line with the medieval Serbian perception that anything resembling paradise had to be "a meadow." Serbian King Stephan the First-Crowned, in his *Chilandar Charter* (1199), called the Holy Mountain a "flatwise sprawling meadow." Stephan's brother, Sava Nemanjich, in his father's biography, *The Life of Saint Simeon* (1208), used the term "the meadow of peace." The "meadow" always abounds in "sweet-voiced birds" which are "super wondrous." This is the place where "desert-loving turtledoves nest." (The term "desert" is used in the sense of a deserted place to where one can withdraw). The natural setting of Mount Athos' "meadow" is truly and "marvelously enhancing." Sava Nemanjic reported that his father "indeed yearned and reposed in this greatly cherished meadow, where birds sang in everchanging voices." He also related how his father "fully satiated himself through five immensely wise senses of seeing, hearing, smelling, vocalizing with, and touching [caressing] the bird."

In the 14th century, the Byzantine theologian, Gregory Palamas (Archbishop of Thessaloniki), wrote that the Holy Mountain had been given to Theotokos by her Son. Emperors, patriarchs, monks and laymen, all treated the Holy Mountain as "The Garden of Panaghia" and "The Shrine of Eastern Christianity." In that sense, the perception of the Holy Mountain as the "earthly paradise" is a vivid and cognizable reality.

No visitor can avoid that impression. Panaghia is present everywhere, participates in everything, and is part of every conversation. Not only does she dominate life on Mount Athos, but her presence excludes the possibility of any other woman being around. Thus, no church on Athos is dedicated to any female saint and, of course, no woman is allowed to step on the soil of the Holy Mountain. The ban on females goes so far as to keep away even female animals which, at least in one field, i.e., transportation, called for the advice of the father of Orthodox monasticism, Saint Theodosios (the Studite). "Try to travel on foot," he said, "as Christ did, but, if there is need, let your beast be the foal of an ass."[2]

Visually, Panaghia's presence is evidenced by innumerable icons of the All-Holy Mother of God. Quite a few of them are said to work wonders. Even if someone undertook the task of listing all the icons of the Panaghia, it would be an exercise in futility. Experts agree that the Mount Athos collection of the Virgin Mary icons has to be the largest in the world, and no one knows how many more are yet to be found.

The wonder-working icons of Panaghia were sometimes given the strangest of names which, once explained, sound considerably less so. Usually, behind the name there is the image of a savior, either of the monastery or the fraternity of monks. The value of the icon is not in the enormity of its salutary power, but in the sincerity and purity of the belief. The artistic presentation radiating from the icon is not what counts, but the fervor of the believer. These icons are among the most precious possessions of the Athonite monastery and objects of greatest veneration. Although images, they are recognized as living persons.

The "PANAGHIA PORTAITISSA" (The Virgin of the Gate) at Iveron is the icon that "walked" over the water from Nicaea to escape persecution. The icon saved the monastery from the evil pirates by warning the monks to lock the gate. Panaghia also caused the pirates' vessels to perish in a stormy sea. The "PANAGHIA PARAMYTHIAS" (The Virgin of Consolation) is said to have done the same thing for Vatopediou when the hegumen was alerted not to open the monastery gate because pirates were lying in ambush. Because Mount Athos monasteries were considered easy prey to numerous mercenary armies and soldiers of fortune in the area, there was a great need for icons that would protect the praying monks.

Panaghia also took care of internal problems that saddled the life of a monk. For instance, both Iveron and Vatopediou went through a period when the olive oil supplies were reduced to naught. Who helped them out but the blessed "PANAGHIA ELIAIOVRYTISSA" (She who flows with oil), by filling at least one of the huge earthen jugs over night.

"PANAGHIA YERONDISSA" (She who has grown old) of the Pantokratoros Monastery so identified with her worshipers that she carried no child in her arms. She is gray-haired, wrinkled and aged just as the elders who run the monastery. At the Philotheou Monastery, the visitor is introduced to the "PANAGHIA GLYKOPHILOUSA" (The Virgin of the Sweet Kiss). She still bears the scar from the sharp dagger of the Islamite, who later repented, became a monk and spent the rest of his life asking forgiveness from the icon. The history of Vatopediou's icon is even more bizarre. In 1822, an angry Turkish soldier shot off the Virgin's hand (THE WOUNDED VIRGIN). Realizing what he had done, the soldier selected the nearest tree and hanged himself. The tree withered the next day.

The Chilandar Monastery has four miraculous Panaghia icons. Two of them are of exceptionally high rank for they were brought by Saint Sava from Jerusalem; he received them as personal gifts from the hegumen of the monastery of Saint Sabba the Sanctified (of Jerusalem). In that monastery, tradition foretold that one day a monk of royal descent from a far away country would arrive at the gate as a pilgrim. His name would be Sava. He was to be given the icon of the Virgin Mary called "MLEKOPITATELNITSA" (She who is nursing by breast). Sava had gone on his first pilgrimage to Jerusalem in 1229. The reason for visiting that particular monastery was another famous icon of the Virgin Mary, the one to which St. John Damascene (c. 675-749) had prayed for restoration of his hand after it had been severed by the executioner. The Virgin Lady took mercy on him and restored his hand. In gratitude, St. John had a hand made of silver which he attached to the icon. Ever since, this icon

has been known as "PANAGHIA TRIKEROUSSA" (The Three-Handed
Virgin Mary) or in the Slavic language, "TROJERUCHITSA".

Sava's arrival was not uneventful. Routinely, every pilgrim first goes
to see the katholikon (main church) of the monastery. As Sava entered
the church, the Pastoral Staff fell off the wall, right in front of Sava's feet!
The astounded ecclesiarch (church steward) rushed to inform the hegumen.
The latter came out and asked the visitor three viable questions: i.e., his
name, lineage and country of origin. Satisfied that the visitor was the person about whom it was prophesied long ago, they gave him the Staff and
two wonder-working icons. Upon his return to the Holy Mountain, Sava
kept the Staff ("Pataritza") in his "House of Silence" (also called "Isichas-
tirion" or "Postnitza" - the Greek and Serbian names for his hermitage in
Karyes). To the adjacent small chapel in Karyes, built for his personal
use, he assigned the icon "Mlekopitatelnitsa" (Galactotrophousa). The
Three-Handed Virgin Lady ("Trojeruchitsa"), he sent to Serbia, to the
Monastery Studenitsa, there to be displayed in times of peace, and to be
carried in front of the Serbian troops in times of war.

Two centuries later, "Trojeruchitsa" miraculously returned to the Holy
Mountain, strapped to the packsaddle of a Providence-guided donkey.
Braving Turkish lookouts, rain and shine, mountains and rivers, the beast
reached Chilandar. Exhausted, it expired before the monks had opened
the gate early in the morning. The monks took the icon into the main
church, but "Trojeruchitsa" refused to remain at the "upper place" assigned in the altar; for three nights in a row she moved to the throne of
the hegumen instead. Finally, "Trojeruchitsa" appeared to the hegumen
in a dream and told him clearly: "Here I came, not to seek your protec-
tion, but to guard you and the monastery!" Since that time, Chilandar
monks elect only the pro-hegumen, and the icon of Trojeruchitsa stands at
the hegumen's throne. This event marked a turning point in the lives of
the Chilandarians. Today, outside the monastery, on the wall of the nearby landmark, the visitor may read the story of the miraculous return of
the icon.

Upon hearing this and other mystical tales, the visitor is well advised to
pause and hold his breath before venturing a comment. It may well prove
to be the crucial moment of his temporary stay with the monks. He has
to make sure he understands the rapport among the monastery, the icon,
and the monk. The visitor cannot expect to be on the same spiritual level
as the monk, because the monk lives on a plane which is unattainable in
a three-day visit. The guest has to make sure he will not venture to judge
his host. The two of them have to part as they had met — as tenants of
two different, if not necessarily opposing, mental abodes.

On the other hand, an art historian may be in the monastery and tell the visitor that actually "Trojeruchitsa" is the work of the 14th century Serbian iconographer. "The iconographic style, inscriptions and particularly the mannerism, trace the icon back to the Serbian art period of King Stefan Dechanski."[3]

A specialist in the history of Mount Athos has stated that the icon was never sent to Studenitsa, as alleged, but to the newly-erected Skoplje Cathedral! He asserts that the icon was "purchased" in Jerusalem. And he says that in 1661, a copy of "Trojeruchitsa" was made in Chilandar at the express wish of the Russian Patriarch Nifon, and was sent to Russia on St. Vitus Day (June 28), a date selected to coincide with the legendary battle of Kosovo.[4]

Today, there are 20 large monasteries — also called "ruling monasteries" — 12 sketes and some 700 kellia on the Holy Mountain. Resident monks of sketes and kellia are considered to be temporary occupants of land and tenements, because according to the Mount Athos Charter the 20 monasteries are the sole real estate owners of the Holy Mountain. No monk can own land on the Holy Mountain. Sketes are made of several kalyvae (dwellings); each skete has a degree of freedom and independence. Resident monks are allowed certain accommodations to meet their own religious needs, suitable to an individual who has difficulty with the strict internal organization of the monastery. Kalyvae monks grow their own vegetables and fruit, some of which they sell and keep the profit for themselves. They paint icons or carve wooden crosses, make rosaries and walking canes. After all, they need the money to pay the rent (to the monastery) because all those sketes belong absolutely and inalienably to the monasteries on which they are dependent.

In the early days, Athonite monasteries went to extra lengths to indicate their rank and standing in relation to other houses of worship. At that time there were many more monasteries on the Holy Mountain than there are today. In his letter to the monks (1214), Pope Innocent III used the term "Heaven's Gate" to describe the Holy Mountain, admitting there were some 300 monasteries on Mount Athos.[5] Classification of a monastery was of utmost importance in terms of freedom of action, business transactions, and ecclesiastical affairs. "The Imperial Monastery," meaning it had been founded by an emperor, was practically untouchable and beyond anybody's jurisdiction. "The Stavropegiac Monastery" had been founded by the will of the patriarch; he placed the cross (stavros) at the building site before the construction began. Jockeying for higher rank and position was important because monasteries patronized by local eparchies and individuals could not avoid being controlled (and taxed) by the local bishop.

Today, the Mount Athos monasteries strictly respect the historical hierarchical ranking as established in the past. The rank is jealously guarded and the listing is always in the same order:

The GREAT LAVRA OF SAINT ATHANASIOS, built in the 10th century, undoubtedly the most eminent shrine of Mount Athos. Serbian medieval rulers generously contributed to the monastery. This is authenticated by the ten Serbian chrysobulls in the library of the monastery. The frescos of the kyriakon (main church) were made by the famous Cretan iconographer Theophanos in 1533. The unusual features of the Lavra are the fresco-portraits of the Greek philosophers Plato, Socrates, Aristotle, Pythagoras, etc. in the monastery's refectory.

VATOPEDIOU, "The Monastery of the Boy and the Bramble-bush," 10th century, was built by three wealthy Adrianopolis citizens. Legend assigns it to Constantine the Great (IV Century). Vatopediou is the only Holy Mountain monastery that has adopted the modern ("Frankish") method of time- keeping, and one of only two which follows the Gregorian calendar. The Serbian monk Sava was joined by his father Nemanya in Vatopediou (1197). The Serbian Despot Ugljesha (14th century) built several structures of the monastery compound, including one chapel. The monastery treasure has the "Girdle of the Virgin" among its precious relics, the gift of the Serbian Princess Militsa, wife of Prince Lazar.

IVERON, "The Monastery of the Iberians," 10th century, was built by the Gruziyan (Georgian) noblemen, John Vazarvache - Tornikios, and his son Athanasios. Moscow's St. Nicholas Monastery was given to Iveron by Tsar Alexei Michailovich.[6] In 1807, Greeks living in Moscow presented the Iveron Monastery with a candelabra in the shape of a lemon tree made of silver and gold.

CHILANDAR, "The Monastery of the Serbs" was built in 1198, on the ruins of the old Greek monastery of the same name (Chelantarion), by Stephan Nemanya and his son Sava. The present katholikon dates from the 14th century, built by King Milutin and Prince Lazar (two churches adjoined) on the site where Nemanya's church formerly stood.

DIONISIOU, 14th century, perched on a cliff 250 feet above the sea, was built by the monk Dionisiou. Generous funding was provided by at least two Byzantine emperors. Later, Moldavian and Wallachian princes supported this monastery.

KOUTLOUMOUSSIOU, dating from the 11th century, was built on the foundations of an older monastery by the converted Seldjuk Prince, Koutloumush. The monastery is adjacent to Karyes, the capital of the Holy Mountain. Prince Koutloumush died in the monastery as Monk Constantine. Saint Sava and Tsar Dushan, as well as Despot Ugljesha, supported Koutloumoussiou.

PANTOKRATOROS, "The Monastery of Christ the Almighty," 14th century, was built by two brothers, both Byzantine noblemen. They intended to retire there as monks, but the monastery burned down the same year it was built (1363). It was later restored by Patriarch Ananios and Emperor John V. Palaeologos. In the 18th century, Catherine the Great of Russia supported Pantokratoros. The big Russian skete of St. Elias belongs to the monastery.

XIROPOTAMOU, "The Monastery of the Dry Torrent," probably founded in the 10th century, was restored by Michael VIII Palaeologos and his heir Andronikos II after pirates incursions and blaze that damaged it in the 13th century. Serbian rulers helped the monastery. Fresco portraits of Nemanya and Sava can be seen in the main church. Xiropotamou almost became extinct in the 18th century, but was saved by alms collected in Moldavia.

ZOGRAPHOU, "The Monastery of the Painter," dedicated to St. George, was built in 1280 by three brothers from Ohrid. Monks were always of Macedonian or Bulgarian origin. The monastery had a turbulent past and was persecuted for opposing Latinization.

DOCHEIARIOU, "The Monastery of the Warden of the Store," built in the 11th century, derived its name from the fact that it was founded by the "docheiaris," Monk Euthimios, formerly of the Great Lavra where he was in charge of food supplies. Tsar Dushan is among the ktytors of the monastery. Rumanian rulers helped the monastery in the days of Turkish rule, ransoming back the monks indebted to Turkish tax collectors.

KARAKALOU, 11th century, was supported by the Palaeologi Andronicos II and John V, and, in the 16th century, by Wallachian Vojvod Petar, who paid off the monastery debts before joining as a monk.

PHILOTHEOU, built in the 11th century, was founded by the hesychast hermit, St. Philotheos, who was St. Athanasios' contemporary. This impoverished monastery was later supported by Tsar Dushan. Serbian and Bulgarian monks were in the majority in the monastery until the beginning of the 17th century. Rumanians took good care of the monastery in the 18th century (Gregory Ghika). In the 19th century, the Russians made an unsuccessful attempt to take over the monastery.

SIMONOPETRA, named after Simonos — building on the rock (petra) — was restored by the Serbian Despot Ugljesha in the 14th century. Monks maintain incorrectly that after Ugljesha's death in the Battle of Maritsa (1371), his son retired to this monastery, became a monk and died there. The monastery is a seven-storied building situated on the rock 1,200 feet high above the water. Serbian monks lived in the monastery until the 18th century. Every year, in October, brethren of the community hold a "parastos" (a special memorial service) for their ktytor, Ugljesha.

SAINT PAUL'S Monastery (named after Saint Paul of Xiropotamou), was restored in the 14th century by two Serbian monks, Gerasim and Antonije. The previous monastery, reduced to the status of kellion, was bought from the Xiropotamou Monastery for 24,000 aspry. The katholikon of the monastery was built by the Serbian Despot Djuradj Brankovic (15th century). His daughter Mara, spouse of Sultan Murad II, maintained a great interest in the monastery. She sent one thousand ducats to the monks and made a precious contribution of the "Gifts of the Magi" (gold, frankincense and myrrh) to the treasury of the monastery. Serbian monks sustained the monastery up to the end of the 17th century.

STAVRONIKITA, 11th century, the monastery of two monks (Stavros and Nikita), was greatly impoverished in the 13th century. At various times it was in the custody of Philotheou, Koutloumoussiou, and Xiropotamou. During the Turkish regime it was supported benevolently by Rumanian vojvods and boyards.

XENOPHONTOS, "The Monastery of the Blessed Xenophon," 11th Century, was rebuilt by the admiral of the fleet of Emperor Nikephoros III. The admiral took his monastic vows in Xenophontos, and was the main donor to the monastery. In the 19th century, the monastery was proclaimed a total loss after a disastrous fire; later it was restored by the Bulgarians.

GRIGORIOU, was founded by Saint Gregory (unclear as to whether he was from Sinai or Syria) in the 14th century. Very little is known about the history of this monastery except that it was generously supported by Moldavian rulers. In the 15th century, it was listed among the Serbian monasteries on the Holy Mountain.

ESPHIGMENOU (called Shimmen or Swimmen as well) the closest neighbor of Chilandar, was built in the 11th century at the very edge of the seashore. It was generously funded by Tsar Dushan and Despot Djuradj Brankovic, (14th and 15th centuries). The miniature family portrait of the latter is preserved in the monastery. Among its monks were such a luminary as Saint Antonii, the founder of Kiev Lavra.

SAINT PANTELEIMONOS, "The Monastery of Russians," was first built in the 12th century by Russian monks who have settled at the Xylourgos skete. They have built the first St. Panteleimonos, now abandoned and known as Paleomonastirion ("The Old Monastery"), high in the mountains. Today's St. Panteleimonos, situated on the coast and of huge proportion, was built in 1765. The monastery compound looks more like a seashore hotel than a monastery. Serbian Saint Sava received the tonsure and donned the "rasson" in the old St. Panteleimonos. Medieval Serbian rulers generously supported the Russian monks on the Holy Mountain, while Chilandar Monastery turned over several sketes to the Russian Monks settling in the area.

KASTAMONITOU was established in the 11th century, and the founder is unknown. Legend has it that the monastery was built by a man from Kastamoni — a Turkish province. In the 15th century, the monastery was restored by the Serbian Vojvod, Radich Postupovich. Among the benefactors still remembered with exceptional gratitude is the Serbian Queen Anne, who donated to the monastery the famous Constantinople icon, "The Virgin Hodeghetria" (Protectress of Travellers). Kastamonitou has a fresco portrait of Saint Sava.

As this abbreviated and condensed presentation of the Mount Athos monasteries indicates, the Serbian presence in the area had not been insignificant in the least. Bearing in mind that the Holy Mountain was part of the Serbian state (in the 14th century), it is only natural that the conquering Serbs tried to endear themselves to the spiritual community which, in many respects, molded Byzantine public opinion.

Archives of the Mount Athos monasteries clearly record the Serbian historical presence and influence in the area. Ornate signatures of Serbian kings and queens, despots, and princes abound in the archives of the Mount Athos monasteries. When the Serbian painter, Dimitrije Avramovich, visited Mount Athos in 1847, he met many of those Serbian ghosts. Impressed, the artist later reported to his nation:" . . . so numerous are those [Serbian] documents that to describe them all, and to give an adequate account, would require one whole book."[7]

Serbian influence in the 13th and 14th centuries was considerable and in effect continued throughout the following two centuries. Document No. 56, dated 1513, as published in the *Acts of Zographou*, mentions no less than seven Slav-speaking hegumens in the Mount Athos monasteries. Five of those monasteries were either founded or restored by Serbian rulers.

Numerous Athonite chrysobulls and edicts that have survived the wear and tear of turbulent centuries display the signatures of Serbian kings and despots. There is Dushan's signature in the Saint Panteleimonos Monastery (1347): "Stephan Dushan, the God-fearing Autocrat of Serbia and Romea" (Romea comprised the Latin-held territories in the Balkans). More modest, although as assertive, is the signature of Prince Lazar in the same monastery, dated 1381: "Honorable Stephen Lazar, Tsar of Serbia." There are signatures that cling to the last vestiges of Serbian medieval power, "Despot Djuradj Brankovic, Ruler of Serbia and Sub-Danubian lands" (Vatopediou, 1453). Note the dignified autograph of Lazar's widow Militsa: "Nun Eugenia, the Princess" (Great Lavra, 1389).

Eight Serbian charters are still on display in Vatopediou: two by Tsar Dushan, three by Despot Ugljesha, two by Despot Djuradj Brankovic, and one by Despot Stephan Lazarevic. The Monastery Esphigmenou has two charters by Dushan, one by Djuradj Brankovic. There are signatures of Dushan in Koutloumoussiou. The Great Lavra has charters signed by Dushan, Tsar Urosh, Lazar, Princess Militsa, and Despot Djuradj Brankovic. Iveron's collection includes two charters by Dushan. Kastamonitou displays the ktytorial charter signed by Vojvod Radich Postupovic, two signed by Despot Djuradj Brankovic, and one by Despot Stephan Lazarevic. It is only understandable that Chilandar proudly displays ten charters by Dushan and 144 by Serbian kings (e.g.- Milutin, Dragutin, Vladislav, Urosh), princes and despots.

The "Serbian period" of the Holy Mountain in the 14th and 15th centuries was so pronounced that the Monasteries Dionisiou, Grigoriou, and Docheiariou were at that time "cited as being Serbian monasteries."[8] Others, like Saint Paul, Simonopetra, and Xenophontos, predominantly Slavic, had a sizeable percentage of Serbian monks as well.

British author F.W. Hasluck points to:

" . . . the growing political influence of the Serbians during the reign of Stephan Dushan and down to the battle of Kosovo (1389) marked by the Serbian foundation of Simonopetra and the revindication of St. Paul's, which is said definitely to be Serbised and made independent of Xiropotamou after Dushan's conquest of Macedonia. There are other traces of Serbian influence, exerted probably about this time, since, in 1489, more than a hundred years later, Isaias [Chilandar monk] cites not only Chilandar and St. Paul's but also Gregoriou, Dionisiou, and Docheiariou as in his time Serbian . . ."[9]

These monasteries later reverted to Greek hands. Hasluck notes that "the process of conversion was probably the same in all cases: the debt-ridden monasteries being bought by rich Greeks"[10]

In terms of internal organization, the Holy Mountain monasteries are of two types: coenobitic ("opshtezhitije") or idiorrhythmic ("osopshtina"). The coenobitic system is known to be very rigorous, and, until recently, run by an autocratic hegumen. The monks live totally impersonal lives as members of a tightly knit religious community. The idiorrhythmic monastic system is considered to be more democratic. Coenobitic is defined as living in a monastery, in a community, governed by monastic rule. Idiorrhythmic is defined as a monastery governed by a deliberative assembly and two or three annually elected presidents — self-governing members, each member regulating his own manner of life.

The hallmark of a coenobitic monastery is the frescoed refectory where monks eat together without conversation, listening to the recital of Scriptures. Among the monks of the coenobitic monastery, the vow of poverty is understood in absolute terms. They have no personal possessions whatsoever; they wear monastery-issued clothes and shoes; they have no private quarters and they are never left alone.

Idiorrhythmic monasteries allow considerable freedom and privacy to their monks. Brethren are allowed to choose to live in one or more rooms of their vast and underpopulated monastery, quarters are cozy and private, monks cook their own food, and purchase whatever they need either at the monastery store or outside. Since they are paid a modest equivalent for services rendered to the monastery, they can, if frugal, save enough money eventually to buy property outside of the Holy Mountain. Refectories in idiorrhythmic monasteries, unlike those in coenobitic monasteries, are used only on feast days; they stay locked most of the time and some are poorly kept. Even attendance at the Church services is not strictly imposed, and an occasional failure to show up is not considered a major breach of routine.

One would expect the monasterial cohesion to suffer under such freedoms. But, apparently, the more liberal options of the idiorrhythmic system became so attractive that the Holy Synod had to forbid switching from a coenobitic system to idiorrhythomy. Yet, reverting to coenobitic status remained always possible. In 1933, Chilandar expressed a desire to return to the coenobitic status, the system explicitly directed by Sava's original *Typikon*. However, the intention fizzled (like the two earlier attempts in the 19th century), allegedly because the Serbian monks insisted that their elected elder ("staratz") be approved by the Serbian hierarchy, rather than by the Greeks.

Today, seven of the 20 ruling monasteries of the Holy Mountain are idiorrhythmic. Of these seven three are amoung the top five monasteries, called "leading monasteries." They happen to be the most prosperous and advanced monasteries of the Holy Mountain (Vatopediou, Iveron and Chilandar).

According to latest listing the two groups include the following monasteries:

Coenobitic monasteries:	Idiorrhythmic monasteries:
Lavra (since 1980)	Chilandar
Dionisiou	Docheiariou
Esphigmenou	Iveron
Gregoriou	Pantokratoros
Karakalou	Philotheou
Kastamonitou	Vatopediou
Koutloumoussiou	Xiropotamou
Simonopetra	
St. Panteleimonos	
St. Paul's	
Stavronikita (since 1968)	
Xenophontos	
Zographou	

Due to trends and influences of modern times, the difference between the two monasterial systems is not as great as it may sound. The image of the autocratic hegumen of the coenobitic monastery is vanishing. He now shares the ruling power with members of the monastery Gerondia (Council of Elders). Although the hegumen is appointed for life, he can be removed if disliked. This may prove to be a tedious process, but it is possible.

As for idiorrhythmic monasteries, they are governed by the Committee of Elders (three or five members). Because the system is known to create a ruling caste of elders, however, such a monastery often ends up with two social strata: the one that rules and the other that is ruled. This is especially true because the majority of monks seem to prefer to leave monastery affairs to those who are better educated.[11]

Differences in daily routine and management of the monasteries are hard to find. Under both systems, duties are assigned to monks in similar fashion, usually on a rotational yearly basis, unless one deals with "specialists," such as the cobbler, wine-maker, fisherman, etc. Certain duties revolve around the liturgical service or upkeep of the Church, and these are rotated per week or month. Librarians tend to hold on to their positions, while duties of guestmasters, porters (gatekeepers), or stewards are shifted around more often.

Of the twenty monasteries on the Holy Mountain, seventeen are held by Greeks. Three — St. Panteleiomonos, Zographou, and Chilandar — are inhabited by monks of Slav descent.

Notes

1. Philipe Sherrard, Athos: *The Holy Mountain* (London, 1982), p.13.
2. ibid., p.22.
3. Dimitrije Bogdanovic, Vojislav J. Djuric, and Dejan Medakovic, *Hilandar* (Belgrade, 1978), p.112.
4. Stanoje Stanojevic, *Enciklopedija*, see Trojerucica entry.
5. Dusan Kasic, *Sveta Gora i Manastir Hilandar* (Belgrade, 1961), p.13.
6. Mateja Matejic. *The Holy Mountain and the Hilandar Monastery* (Columbus, Ohio, 1983), p.24.
7. Dimitrije Avramovic, *Opisanie drevnosti srbski u Svetoi (Atonskoi) gori s XIII litografisani tablica* (Belgrade, 1847).
8. Sherrard, *Athos,* p.32.
9. Hasluck, F. W., *Athos and its Monasteries* (London, 1924), p.56.
10. ibid., p.57
11. Emmanuel Amand de Mendieta, *Mount Athos, The Garden of Panaghia* (Berlin, 1972), p.101.

Chapter II

KARYES: GATEWAY TO THE HOLY MOUNTAIN

The capital of the Monastic Republic of Mount Athos is the small sleepy town called Karyes. It owes its name, many believe, to its hinterland, the lush vegetation of hazelnut and walnut trees. In the old Serbian documents the town was often referred to as Orahovitsa (The City of Walnuts). It is easy to view it as a cross between a county seat and a ghost town. Most of the time its single street is deserted. Heavy wooden shutters seal all openings, such as entrances, doorways, windows, and other means of access to structural cavities. The venerated little capital can be reached by bus, the only one that operates on the peninsula. It picks up the mail and the visitors in the coastal village of Daphne, named after the daughter of the king of ancient Arcadia.

Luggage in hand, the visitor has no other choice but to venture down the stone-paved lane, hoping against hope to meet a living soul or at least to find a shaded spot. After a very short walk, the visitor reaches the "downtown" area, a treeless plaza featuring a basilica-type temple and the adjacent tall "pyrgos" (tower) serving as the bell tower. The temple is the oldest church of the Holy Mountain, an imposing 10th-century structure, dedicated to the Dormition of the Blessed Virgin, locally known as the Church of Protaton. The Protaton is the residence of the Protos, the building opposite the church. In the 14th century, Byzantine Emperor Andronikos (1286-1328) and his contemporary, King Milutin of Serbia (1282-1321), who, for a while was the Emperor's son-in-law, pooled resources and decorated the church with frescoes. Art historians maintain that some of the frescoes (still preserved) were done by the leading artist of the Macedonian School, Manuel Panselinos.

Life returns to the city almost inaudibly. First, the silhouette of a bearded monk is seen stepping out from the shaded side of the tall tower, quickly disappearing under the arched porch of the Church. Then, faint sounds of hushed conversation in narrow alleys, converging on the town's plaza in a spoke-like fashion, indicate some commotion. Finally, one hears the distinct mule's hoofs clap. Dismounting their beasts, still communicating in subdued voices, arriving monks appear from all sides of the town, and enter the famous Church, the one that harbors the most revered of all Athonite Virgin Ladies, the "Axion Estin" (The Praiseworthy).

Since Karyes is the administrative center of the Holy Community of Mount Athos, all visitors to the Mountain have to come here to obtain a permit - diamonitirion - to stay overnight in monasteries of their choice. The simple procedure that takes place in the hall of the Protaton makes it very clear that after three nights the visitor has exhausted the hospitality of the Holy Mountain. The residence of the Protos (Primus) is an imposing building, its wide stairway and cool vast hall unerringly conveying the sense of salvation from the summer heat. The sight of the banner emblazoned with the Byzantine two-headed eagle reminds the visitor of a different world that existed here.

Today, Karyes is a meeting place of genuine parliamentarians. Monks assembling for vesper services in their beloved Church are, in fact, elected delegates of their respective monasteries. Here they are on a one year assignment to help govern their monastic community. They live in town, in houses called "kellion," minding community affairs but never forgetting to pay their dues to the Deity, the essential part of their monastic vow. Delegates serve as "ambassadors" of their monasterial constituencies and, in that sense, the narrow alley descending toward the center of the capital may be considered an "embassy row."

Monks take their governmental duties very seriously. Timid as they may look, they have proved to be impressively assertive on occasion. In 1662, they forced the Patriarch to redefine the autocratic authority of the Protos. Their opposition to centralization and respect for adversary democracy prompted the western humanist Sir Thomas More to make the Mount Athos system a model for his own vision of an ideal society, when writing his famous treatise *Utopia* in 1516. Mount Athos' past is replete with healthy tensions, internal struggles and disputes - whether of doctrinal, administrative, or even political nature - indicating that seemingly conformist monks cherish their independence and freedom of action.

The resolution of the problem of ironing out all internal inadequacies of the monastic system took several centuries and six major amendments of the Mount Athos Typikon by ecumenical patriarchs. The self-government, as practiced today, is the one decreed by Patriarch Gabriel IV in 1783 — the Sixth Typikon. In order to give each monastery a chance to participate in the governing process, the 20 monasteries were grouped in five tetrads (groups of four monasteries). The monastery listed at the head of each tetrad was called the "leading monastery." In practice, this meant that the delegate of the leading monastery acted as the leader of his group. By the same token, he would become the head of the entire monastic community and, in fact, assumed the duty of the Protos in the year when his group was in charge of governing. The rotational system was to guarantee each monastery this supreme honor every fifth year.

Chilandar is the leading monastery of the fourth tetrad, consisting of Chilandar, Xiropotamou, St. Paul's and Gregoriou. Every fifth year, delegates of the fourth tetrad make up the Epistasia, which is the executive body of Mount Athos's General Assembly (Synoxis). They are known as "epistates," while the delegate of Chilandar, as first among equals, becomes "Protepistatis."

In this capacity, the delegate acts as the Premier ("Protos") of the monastic republic. The symbol of his temporary authority is the ebony-made Pastoral Staff, topped with a silver knob. The Medal of the Panaghia and the cross worn around his neck, as well as the assigned constumed seimenis, his personal guard, add to the Protos's prestige. (The guard should not be taken for a member of the local gendarmerie, i.e., of the Greek state police.)

Today, apart from being the capital of monks, Karyes is the seat of the Greek Government envoy as well, although he has little influence upon monasterial affairs on Mount Athos. His main duty consists of protecting the monks from the intrusion of outsiders. Unless a Byzantologist himself, the governor would find little else to do in Karyes but to fight boredom, just as numerous Turkish kaimakams have done before him.

In addition to discharging the duties of the Protos, the head of the Monastic Republic simultaneously runs the affairs of the town. As Karyes' Mayor he becomes involved in issuing numerous ordinances, such as the ban on smoking, singing, or dancing in the street, price control, and sale of meat on certain days.

The authority of the Assembly in Karyes is precisely defined by the Charter of the Holy Mountain and, while one can say that this body rules over the monasteries, it certainly cannot govern in such a way as to interfere with the self-managing rights of each monastery. In most of the cases, the Assembly either assists a monastery in financial straits or acts as moderator in occasional inter-monasterial disputes. Directives of the Assembly must be carried out by the monastery which in turn retains the right of appeal to the ecumenical patriarch.

As the much-revered capital of Mount Athos, Karyes holds a special place in the hearts of traditionalist Serbs. At the very beginning of the

13th century, in this idylic town, Sava Nemanjic had built himself a kellion; he called it a small "sedishte" (nook). He chose the site of the retreat
personally at the time when he had made the decision to live in solitude,
the life of an ascetic. Among Slavs, kellions of this kind were known
under the general term of m'lchalnitsa (House of Silence); there the occupant had no one to talk to and could meditate, "in prayers and tears to
serve Jesus Christ one on one, day and night" - as Sava's grandnephew
King Milutin defined it later (1318).

However, events and developments on Mount Athos as well as abroad,
notably in Serbia, prevented Sava from achieving his goal. Basically,
Sava-the-hermit never ceased to be Sava-the-public-man. He never lost
sight of or interest in his monastery nor of his nation. The vicinity of the
Protos' office undoubtedly was a factor in Sava's decision to reside in
Karyes. Frequently, at the express request of the Protos, Sava went to
Thessaloniki, there he was to represent the entire Holy Community in mat-
ters of great importance.

As business demanded a need to stay in the city of Thessaloniki for extended periods, Sava decided to secure for himself a base in this famous
city. The Philocalos Monastery, in ruins ever since the Normans damaged
it in 1183, seemed to be an appropriate place. Sava restored the monastery
and gave Philocalos a pronounced Serbian touch. Serbian monks and
travellers, for many years commuting between the Holy Mountain and
their homeland, found a snug shelter in Philocalos.

Maintaining his base in Karyes (1200-1208), in his tiny cave-like cubicle
adjacent to the small chapel, Sava would regularly visit the Chilandar
Monastery for Sunday liturgical services, there to pray in the church built
by Nemanya, and to talk "shop" with the first hegumen of Chilandar,
Metodije. The distance between Karyes and Chilandar is a good six-hour
walk. On one such visit, Metodije informed Sava of the miracle that had
taken place in the monastery: myrrh-oil was found to be flowing from the
body of Sava's late father Nemanya. It goes without saying that an event
like this could not have passed unnoticed among the monks of the Holy
Mountain; they took it as a positive sign of Nemanya's sainthood.

Apparently Sava's sojourn in Karyes left a mark in the history of Mount
Athos monasticism. He appeared to be a monastic fundamentalist, striving to return to the origins of a hermetic life style and of asceticism.

To live the scrupulous and strict life of an Athonite kelliot was not enough
for Sava. Going a step further, Sava brought to Karyes the authenticity
of the ascetic style of Jerusalemian monasticism, at variance with the
redominant Byzantine monasticism of the time. Sava formulated his views
on ascenticism in the *Karyes Typikon* (1199), the statute he wrote for his

kellion, and the small Chapel dedicated to St. Sabba the Sanctified (of Jerusalem).

Occupants of Sava's kellion in Karyes live by these rigorous ascetic rules, considered to be the most austere and demanding in the entire Holy Mountain. Monks living in Sava's kellion were hermits of lean flesh, worn to the bones, but giants of spirit. Professor Aleksandar Deroko,in his book on Mount Athos, describes the hermit he met there as:

> ...a single monk, who conducts continuous day and night services completely alone. He washes the stone floor of the small chapel, pulls at the rope of the bell, and looks after his house himself. He has very little time to sleep or to rest, observes the most rigorous fasts - all this at over eighty years of age." [1]

Sava wrote his set of rules on parchment, preserved in Chilandar until today. "I installed here in Orahovitsa this place of silence (m'lchalnitsa)," writes Sava in his *Typikon* "and I am establishing this statute to be upheld in this kellion by the one who wants to live here: On Mondays, Wednesdays, and Fridays, eat no oil, nor drink wine...and on all five days eat only once a day.   In the Liturgy, let the statute be upheld in this manner: for morning services and vespers, proceed as is customary, but morning services should include readings of three kathismae of the Psalter throughout the year, while evening services should carry the Prayer to the Lord without a troparion...the final stage of the evening service should be when the words 'God have mercy upon us', and 'bless us O Lord' are spoken to include twelve prostrations."

The *Typikon* specifies in detail the obligations of the Chilandar Monastery toward its dependency, Sava's kellion in Karyes. For instance, it states: "There ought to be given sixty liters of oil for the vigil light to Saint Sabba the Sanctified (of Jerusalem) per year." Then there are instructions which sound more like pleading than giving explicit orders: "I am beseeching the hegumen and the brethren not to forget the man living in this kellion, I myself am hoping that a handful of flour and a cup of oil will not be lacking on your part, if you wish to have my, though sinful, supplication coming to you." Sava points out to kellion's independent status "...to all of you let it be known: neither the Protos, nor the hegumen of the holy monastery or anyone of the brothers should ever bother the person living there." Finally, Sava implores the resident monk. "... not to change anything written in here, and may no one dare to remove a single book or icon; one who does it, let him be damned."

Apparently, resident monks took Sava's instructions very seriously. One kelliot went so far as to have the Typikon carved in stone; he then affixed the slab over the door for anyone to read. Because of "Russianisms" noticeable in the shorthand inscription, some experts believe, the resident monk must have been of Russian nationality. Whoever he was, he gave a new name to the "House of Silence." At that time (beginning in the 19th century) Sava's kellion became "The House of the Typikon" ("Tipikarnitsa").

Sava's kellion was not spared of its share of destruction and distress when bad times befell the Holy Mountain. One particularly difficult period was in the beginning of the 14th century when Karyes was pillaged by intruders. The kellion was heavily damaged and depleted of basic requirements necessary for normal functioning. In those horrid and excruciating times, the Chilandar Monastery, struggling for its own survival, could not be of any assistance to the kelliot in Karyes.

Two concerned Chilandarians, the hegumen of the monastery and the resident of the kellion, Nikodim and Theodul, decided that grieving and lamenting were of no use. They headed for a long trip north, in search of the famous Serbian King, known for his readiness to make the monks' cause one of his own. Such a king was the awesome Milutin, who in his lifetime had built or restored more churches than all other Serbian kings together.

In his subsequent "Karyes Kellion Charter" (1318), the resolute King gave us the details of his meeting with the two Athonites. As they arrived, the monks stated their business, submitted a direct plea for help, and especially emphasized the need to restore Sava's damaged and plundered kellion in Karyes. The sovereign's reply was just as plain and factual: "...whatever the holy elder, Kyr Theodul, said he needed, I gave, for the restoration and for the continual upkeep of the kellion of my royal ancestor, Saint Sava; I replenished it with books and holy icons and all other necessities." [2]

The King deposited 1,000 perpers with the monastery to cover expenses for the support of the kellion and demanded that Chilandar's Council of Elders pledge "to provide the (Karyes) kelliots with two metrics of bread and oil and lentils and with garb and footwear, as long as this Holy Mountain and this monastery of ours stands; as for wine no giving is required." [3]

In his Charter King Milutin reminded the hegumen that it was the obligation of the monastery not to forget the original demand of Sava (to whom Milutin referred as "Saint Sava, the Forefather of the Kingdom.") to provide the sixty liters of oil for the vigil-light.

Then the King reminded the hegumen of another request stipulated in the Typikon of the Karyes kellion by its founder—the absolute sanctity of the kellion's independence and the requirement not to interfere with the life of the kelliot.

Subsequently, the King signed the Karyes Charter in scarlet. The signature was placed below the usual clause: "This I wrote, and this I confirm with the Golden Seal." Though merely a king, Milutin used an imperial mark of authority when he signed: "Stephan Urosh, by the Grace of God the King, with the Lord's help, the Autocrat of lands Serbian and of the Littoral."

To make sure his royal orders would be obeyed, King Milutin insisted that this particular document be co-signed by a host of guarantors: the Holy Mountain Protos Isaac, Chilandar's hegumen Nikodim, Chilandar's confessor ("bashta") Arsenije, the King's own confessor Joasaf, and the monastery elders as per their rank — all of those signatures to be placed "underneath the imperial markings of my own..."

Thirty years later, the Serbian imperial couple, Dushan and his Bulgarian wife Jelena, arrived at the Holy Mountain. They spent the winter there (1347-1348). Dushan had visited many athonite monasteries, but Jelena, out of consideration for the sensitivity of the anti-female sequestered community of monks, visited only a few. However, she did go to Sava's famous "m'lchalnitsa" in Karyes which she found to be in deplorable condition. Major restoration was needed as well as more reliable support than the one which the monastery was able to give. The wretched destiny of the now veteran ascetic Theodul must have moved the Empress deeply. There on the spot she offered to become the patroness of St. Sava's kellion and reaffirmed Theodul as the "lifelong elder of the hermitage." Then she goaded her husband to bestow the Karyes kellion with a landed estate in Serbia. Today, it is hard to envision Theodul as a feudal landlord. The devout monk had to find time to worry about "the village Kosoriche in Hvosno, and its entire landed estate...this including all portions, vineyards and water mills, meadows, pastures, forest clearings and the mountain as a whole." [4]

Could Sava ever have foreseen that a woman, Bulgarian by birth, would become the ktytor of his kellion? Worse yet, that the resident monk of "m'lchalnitsa", apart from Psalters and holy books, would have to busy himself with account books and balance sheets?

It did not take long before the ktytorship of Empress Jelena was challenged by Chilandarians. Her husband, Tsar Dushan, had been dead for four years when the Chilandar Elders gathered to elect the new lifelong resident of the kellion in Karyes. Normally, an empress-ktytor would have been informed of the coming procedure and sounded out on the candidate. Chilandarians, however, decided first to elect an Elder (Mihailo) for the kellion, and inform Jelena about their selection only after the fact. One wonders: was it because at that time Jelena was not an empress any more, but merely nun-Jelisaveta? Or was it because, as the Chilandarians respectfully stated in their letter, "Sava always wanted it this way?"

Today, the resident of Sava's kellion is the young Chilandarian Serafim. Tall and lean, he is in his late twenties; his bulging blue eyeballs focus on his finger work as he endlessly ties and unties the knots of his woolen rosary. To an outsider, young Serafim projects an air of a mystic. Envision Monk Serafim in the Kellion's crypt pointing to the skull of the previous kelliot. For a fleeting moment, he may easily bring to mind the image of the young Danish prince immortalized by Shakespeare. In the darkness of the underground vault, Serafim stares at the hollow cranium on the shelf: "This is Elder Dimitrije. He was eighty-six years old when he died here...You know, Chilandar is like a ship: certain people come on board but soon go ashore, whereas others stay on to the end of their lives. Dimitrije made port here - God bless his soul — I myself dug him out a year ago." To think that young Serafim will "make port" here as well, inasmuch as the resident of Sava's kellion is elected for life.

Seldom does Serafim venture to "downtown" Karyes. He grows his own vegetables on the richly composed walled-in plot, only a step away from Sava's chapel. Obviously, food is of no concern to the kelliot. In late October, sackfuls of ripe apples and plums litter the ground begging to be collected before busy bees turn them into honey, or a combination of rot, mold, and warm sun rays initiates the process of fermentation and decay. "This is God's pleasure," muses Serafim, recalling St. John's diet in the desert. "He ate grasshoppers," Serafim would say pointedly, and then add rather wryly: "Of course, jumbo-size grasshoppers!..."

Satisfied that his wit has startled the guest, the pale hermit moves for a final knock: "You know, my most fervent wish was to follow in the steps of St. John. I came to the Holy Mountain because Sava repeatedly referred to Mount Athos as a 'desert,' the 'earthly paradise'... I came here only to discover that the Holy Mountain 'desert' is a 'tourist paradise!'."

Leaving the "House of Silence" to its occupant, the visitor continues to walk up the steep narrow alley to the three-storied building locally known as "Chilandar's konakion." Its spacious vine-arbored terrace offers a magnificent bird's-eye view of the tiny capital below. The adjacent Koutloumoussiou Monastery seems to be at arm's reach, and the overall vista sweeps above the treetops of surrounding hills all the way to the blue sea. Down there, the Iveron Monastery embellishes the beauty of the coastline.

In no time, caretaker Vita appears. The jingling tray in his hands epitomizes the opening stage of a visit to any Holy Mountain monastery. The obligatory tall glass, of cool spring water, the cube of "Turkish Delight," and the coffeepot ("dzezva") of steaming coffee — this is the first of the many triads the visitor will encounter on the Holy Mountain.

Vita is an older man, in his 60's, hard of hearing and a widower living in Great Britain. He comes to Karyes for an extended stay every summer. "The monastery is in permanent need of a handy man," he may volunteer before returning to whatever he was doing. Among the Chilandarians, Vita is known as the Godsent "Mr. Fix-it."

Being an outsider and a layman, Vita feels free to evaluate the monastic life for an inquisitive stranger. He perceives the monastery in terms of housekeeping.

"Everything depends on the hegumen," he says, because "basically, the monastery is like a household." Most taxing of the many monastic requirements—in his opinion—"are long prayer hours, starting at 2 a.m. Long prayers regenerate the elders, but wear out the novices and younger monks.... For some reason, the elders either cannot or do not know how to shorten the prayer periods...thus they are losing many valuable men, all of those who come here and pray and pray endlessly, until one day, they leave abruptly...some may come back after a while, but only to leave for good...."

Quite different is the tenant of the Chilandar konakion, Father Mitrofan, a seasoned monk of the Holy Mountain, and a missionary with worldly connections.

He is the Public Relations person of Chilandar. Also, he is the editor of Chilandar's publication (*Hilandar*) and an evangelist who keeps the mystic symbolism of his monastery alive in every corner of the Serbian Diaspora all over the world. The most travelled of all Chilandarians, he is well known among the Serbian "guest workers" in Europe, the emigres in the North American continent, as well as among numerous Serbs who settled in Australia. In this respect, he continues to carry out the traditional missionary work of famous 16th and 17th century Chilandarians, who dared to venture as far away as Moscow or Trieste.

Mitrofan is one of the best informed Chilandarians today. This may tempt the guest to ask many questions, thereby losing many hours of needed overnight rest, before starting the grueling hike to Chilandar early the next morning.

NOTES

1. Aleksandar Deroko, Mount Athos (*Belgrade*), p.19.
2. Vladimir Mosin, Povelje Kralja Milutina Karejskoj celiji, 1318, Glasnik Skopskog naucnog drustva 19, (Skoplje, 1938), p.59.
3. ibid., p.60.
4. Radoslav Grujic, Carica Jelena i celija Sv. Save u Kareji, Glasnik Skopskog naucnog drustva 14, (Skoplje 1935), p.51.

Chapter III

THE FOUNDERS OF CHILANDAR

Sava and Nemanya reached the Holy Mountain six years apart — Sava in 1191, as nineteen year-old Prince Rastko, a runaway, a dreamer and an idealist, and Nemanya in 1197, at that time a Studenitsa monk, former Grand Zhupan of Rascia (Serbia), world-wise, and experienced in Byzantine customs and exercises. Different as they were, they had but one ideal — to build a Serbian monastery there.

While still in Serbia, Prince Rastko, the youngest of Nemanya's three sons, had an opportunity to meet numerous monastics who were visiting his father's court. Sava was a well-read youngster, familiar with vitae of the holy men of Orthodoxy. Visitors impressed him and books fascinated him; clearly he was not a person whom the life-style of a courtier would please. Before long, he seriously contemplated the idea of leaving the court. What kept him back was the thought that his intention would destroy the elderly parents who loved him dearly.

Ratsko's dilemma was solved by a Russian monk, visiting from the Holy Mountain. The monk knew how to talk to the romantic youngster. One day, as patricians and courtiers of noble birth were tracking and stalking big game, the two friends left the hunting party inconspicuously.

Upon being told of his son's disappearance, Nemanya correctly assumed that Rastko must have headed south. The posse was sent immediately to fetch the Prince. But the well-travelled and cunning Russian monk, using back roads and roundabout ways, knew how to cover their tracks. All the way down to Thessaloniki and beyond, the captain of the posse found no trace of the two fugitives. When he finally caught up with his Prince, the royal runaway was in the custody of the Monastery St. Panteleimonos on the Holy Mountain. At first, the captain tried to reason with his Prince, hoping Rastko would abandon his original idea. Then he appealed to Rastko not to hurt his aged parents. Throughout this conversation the cap-

tain was at a disadvantage, he standing below in the courtyard of the
monastery and Rastko talking from high above on the parapet of the
monastery pyrgos. They finally agreed to "sleep on" the decision. The
next morning the distraught captain was faced with a harsh reality, when
Rastko threw his hunting suit and a tuft of shorn hair." Take this to my
parents, " he yelled " and tell them you saw their son in the rasson of
the monk, as of now named Sava." In his anguish, the tired soldier could
only mumble:" First, he deceived his father, now myself!" Then he let
his soldiers vent their rage upon the monks. This account of the event is
given by Sava's biographer Teodosije.[1]

Today, at the site of the old St. Panteleimonos, the famous pyrgos still
stands, although an extensive restoration of the monastery took place in
1871. Along with the entire block of kellia that were rebuilt, one chapel
was erected and dedicated to Sava of Serbia. The altar of the present small
Church stands at the very spot where once stood the Chapel of Saint John
the Forerunner, this being the chapel where "the Serbian Prince was
clothed in the monk's garb and shorn the first time." [2]

Sava arrived in the Spring of 1191. The news that a Slav prince had
joined the brethren of St. Panteleimonos quite naturally created excitement
among the Athonites. Many wanted to catch a glimpse of the newcomer,
others invited him to visit, and still others tried to lure him to move into
their monastery. Undoubtedly, a person of such high status would greatly enhance the rank of the monastery. Eventually, Sava agreed to attend
the feast-day ("slava") of the Monastery Vatopediou (Annunciation, April
7th, Gregorian calendar). Once there, Sava decided not to return to St.
Panteleimonos. History has not recorded what caused him to stay, but
anyone who had the fortune to visit Vatopediou can understand: the
monastery is captivating both visually and spiritually.

Sava lived some five years in Vatopediou before his father joined him.
His generosity is well recorded in the monastery. Sava built three chapels
in Vatopediou. He had the roof of the katholikon covered with leaden
plates. He restored the Church of St. Simeon in Prosphora, a dependency
of Vatopediou. Prior to the reunion of father and son, Sava gave a great
deal of gold to the monastery. That was to cover the expenses of feeding
and lodging the party of some 50 artisans and craftsmen sent by Nemanya.
The fact that Sava had all these funds at his disposal clearly indicated that
the royal parents were supportive of their son, and that Nemanya was soon
to join Sava.

Meanwhile in Serbia, Nemanya had decided to abdicate (1196). Both
his age and pressing politics must have influenced his decision to withdraw
from public life. At that time Alexios III Angelos (1195-1203) became

the Emperor of Byzantium. His daughter had married Nemanya's second oldest son Stephan (later King Stephan the First-Crowned). The Emperor wanted his daughter to be the Serbian Queen, not the wife of the possible heir. Besides, Nemanya was having some bad luck with the Byzantines; he had fought unfortunate battles and had suffered devastating setbacks.

Upon retiring, Nemanya withdrew to his own monastery, Studenitsa, in Serbia, where he dedicated his time to reading, praying, and fasting. There he became a monk of senior rank (Megaloschemos, Wearer of Great Habit) and was given the name of Simeon. After eighteen months in the monastery in Serbia, he decided to yield to Sava's constant urging to join him at the Holy Mountain. Nemanya started his journey on October 8, 1197.

He reached Vatopediou on November 2nd. Nemanya arrived laden with gifts for everyone: rich gifts for the Protos, separate gifts for the host-monastery Vatopediou. Also, Nemanya brought along dozens of animals, strong mules and horses, a highly-appreciated requisite on the Mountain.

In his biographical essay about his parent, Sava describes the father-son encounter in the following words: ". . . He [Nemanya] arrived on the Holy Mountain on the second day of November. First he settled in the Vatopediou Monastery, where he found his cherished prodigal sheep. . ." What an extraordinary relationship: the shepherd abandoning his herd to be with the sheep that wandered away; also, the Grand Zhupan and monk of higher rank, submitting to the pastorate of the son, a monk of lower rank.

This was more than a meeting between father and son; above all it was a meeting of two determined monks committed to building a Serbian monastery on this holy soil of Eastern Orthodox Christianity. Relentlessly and with unending dedication, they explored the Holy Mountain, looking for a suitable location. Wandering around they visited numerous monasteries and became "second ktytors" of Iveron and Great Lavra, as well as of the Protaton Church in Karyes. In Vatopediou, according to biographer Teodosije, they had the refectory enlarged, and the walls decorated with new frescoes.

Journeys of this kind, over the difficult landscape of Mount Athos, were not at all easy for the aged Nemanya. More often than not he had to be carried on a stretcher, mounted between two docile mules. But the old man persevered; he being "the father obedient to the son," Nemanya (83), "the snow-white winter," and Sava (26) "the blossoming Spring." [3]

Finally, they found a place to their liking. The gentle valley, its olive groves opening to the idyllic gulf, on the region called Mileie, caught Nemanya's eye. Seeing the ruins of an old monastery, he felt any further search to be needless. The ruins of the old building were those of the Greek Monastery Chelantarion, which was known to exist there in the 10th century. Old Mount Athos documents carry the signature of a certain George Chelandarios ("boatman"), a ranking Athonite in his time, and "probably the founder of the monastery, which was subsequently named after him." [4]

Losing no time, Nemanya and Sava undertook the necessary steps to obtain permission to build the monastery. This required some lobbying in Karyes, a trip to Constantinople, and considerable persuasiveness in dealing with the Vatopediou hegumen. Because Chelantarion was in the custody of Vatopediou, its hegumen had to agree to the transfer of property, but he was reluctant to do so. Vatopediouians, in general, were not thrilled by the idea of losing the attention of two generous Serbs. Finally the hegumen reasoned that, in the long run, it was better to let them go and part as friends.

In Karyes, the Protos had no objection to Nemanya's plan. Noblemen with interest in the Holy Mountain were always welcome in his office. In Constantinople, the ruling emperor was Alexios III, the "father-in-law" ; he was more than glad to see Nemanya give up the throne and readily endorsed Nemanya's request to build a monastery on the Holy Mountain and to retire there.

When Sava came to Constantinople to obtain the blessing of the Patriarch and the gold-sealed charter signed by the Emperor, his assignment turned out to be a mere breeze. While waiting to be received in audience, and subsequently for the documents to be issued, Sava stayed in the famous Constantinople Monastery of the Holy Virgin, the Evergetis (Benefactress), which both Nemanya and Sava had supported and helped generously.

The decisive document that Sava obtained from the Emperor stated that Nemanya and Sava "...intend to restore, in fact, build anew, a monastery that will serve the religious needs of men of Serbian nationality" [5]. The new monastery was to be a gift to the Serbs "in perpetuity." Neither the Protos nor anyone else should have any authority over the monastery. As a token of imperial authority, Alexios III sent to the hegumen of the monastery the "imperial staff," to be kept there and attest to the highest rank of the monastery, the rank of an "imperial monastery" ("tsarska lavra").

This meant that Chilandar was to be on the same level as the Monasteries Iveron, Meghisti Lavra, and Vatopediou. Also, the Serbian Chilandar was given possession of several metochia (land properties), smaller monasteries, sketes and kellions as requested by Sava. Later, in the same year

(1198), Nemanya issued his own gold-sealed Chilandar Charter, making the monastery a hereditary foundation of the Nemanjic dynasty.

Feeling weak and old, Nemanya was in a hurry to settle all matters pertaining to the legal status of Chilandar as quickly as possible. Consequently, he asked his son Stephan - at that time the actual ruler of Serbia - to affirm his own patronage over Chilandar, regardless of the fact that Nemanya was still alive. Stephan responded by sending substantial financial aid and whatever material was necessary for the completion of the monastery. Thus, Stephan figured as "second ktytor" of Chilandar as Nemanya's partner. Later, Stephan was to write his own founding charter for Chilandar.

As for the progress of work on the building site, scholars agree that no time was wasted and that there was no shortage of professional expertise either. Serbian craftsmen that were kept by Sava in Vatopediou, as well as draft animals brought by Nemanya, were all moved to the construction site and put to good use. According to Professor Nenadovic, an expert in medieval restoration, and in charge of Chilandar's present restoration, the work advanced surprisingly fast.

> The very short time period, hardly more than a year in which they [Nemanya and Sava] built their monastery Hilandar, indicated that the old monastery was probably not razed to the ground, and that the use of old materials must have been substantial; primarily stone blocks belonging to the former Helantarion. This also suggests that the first Church of Hilandar was not of large proportions....[6]

In this same short period other buildings were finished; those that served as refectory and kitchen, as well as those used for sheltering the monks or as guest quarters. The solid protective wall with a massive pyrgos was erected as part of the first monastery compound.

Nemanya moved into the monastery in May of 1199. At the very outset, the monastery's katholikon was dedicated to the Presentation of the Virgin in the Temple, while the monastery Chilandar was consecrated to the Virgin Hodeghetria ("The one who shows the road"). Historians do not agree on how long Nemanya lived in his monastery. However, most of them believe that he died by the end of 1199, i.e., after a period of eight months in Chilandar, not 16 as was assumed previously.

In this short period of time, or as biographer Domentian puts it, "before the time arrived for him to give to the Lord his due," Nemanya made sure the patronage (ktytorship) of the Mount Athos monastery had passed onto his son Stephan. In the *Chilandar Founding Charter* of 1198, Nemanya had clearly indicated this intent of his when he wrote:" . . .so you [Stephan] have it, and your children and grandchildren, and your offspring and your lineage...." Stephan, for his part, found it necessary to write in his own *Chilandar Charter* of 1199 the following:" I was granted the honor of sharing the duty of the ktytor with him [Nemanya], and of becoming the servant of the monastery, by donating villages (list of ten), a mountain (one), vineyards (two) and a trading post (one). To this I later added . ."

In Chilandar, Nemanya died lying on the straw mat in the narthex of the very Church he built, with the patronal icon of the Virgin Lady Hodeghetria by his head. He was buried in the Church. However, in 1195, Nemanya had already secured for himself a burial place in Serbia, in the Studenitsa Monastery. So strong was his desire to lie in Serbian ground, that on his dying bed, he implored Sava to make sure his remains would be taken back to Serbia one day. Then, in a hardly audible whisper, he added," And now, my son, my soul is in fearful need of thy prayers."

NOTES

1. For the historians' version of the same episode, see Stanoje Stanojevic, O *dolasku* Sv. Save u manastir, Svetosavski Zbornik, Vol. I, Belgrade, 1936).

2. Putevoditel po Svjatoi Afonskoi Gore, (Odessa, 1902), p.36.

3. Nicholai D. Velimirovic, The Life of St. Sava, (Libertyville, Ill., 1951), p.38.

4. Mirjana Zivojinovic, Manastir Hilandar i Mileje, Hilandarski zbornik IV p.8.

5. Cedomir S. Draskovic, Hiljadugodisnjica Svete Gore i njen znacaj za pravoslavlje (The Holy Mountain millenium volume) (Belgrade 1961), p.10.

6. Slobodan Nenadovic, Arhitektura Hilandara, crkve i paraklisi, Hilandarski zbornik III, (Belgrade 1974), p.88.

Chapter IV

THE TYPIKON

Sava must have been the most talked about monk of the Holy Mountain. With direct lines of contact to the courts of Byzantium and Serbia, he was the darling of the hegumens and of the Protos. Intent on helping and always ready to mediate for the sake of his fellow Athonites, Sava was one of the busiest monks of the community. One wonders how he found time and energy to care for his own Chilandar as much as he did.

Once the actual construction of his monastery was completed, Sava had to make sure that all that masonry did not remain an empty shell. Predestined to be the spiritual leader of his people, Sava now worked on making the Chilandar Monastery the spiritual center of Serbia.

He brought more people into the monastery. What started as a brotherhood of 16 monks, shortly grew to 90. Quite a few of them were Athonites, living in nearby monasteries; others came from Serbia. Once established, Chilandar had an average of 150 resident monks on a yearly basis.

Another matter that required Sava's immediate attention was the monastery bylaws, a set of practical regulations affecting duties and obligations, as well as rights, of the monks. For a statute of this kind, Sava drew the *Typikon* for Chilandar by adapting the bylaws of the Monastery of the Virgin Mary the Evergetis, at that time the most famous monastery in Constantinople. The *Typikon* was of a coenobitic kind, requiring rigid discipline, obedience to the hegumen, and total abandonment of private life. The daily routine of a coenobitic monk is strenuous, demanding absolute adherence to the vows of obedience, poverty, and chastity. Both Sava and Nemanya preferred the coenobitic organization to the idiorrhythmic, as they saw the former at work in other monasteries they knew so well. Sava used to stay in the Monastery of the Virgin Mary the Evergetis whenever he was in Constantinople. As for Nemanya, the circumstances were somewhat less fortunate, in view of the fact that he was kept in Constantinople under house arrest for rebelling against the Emperor (1172). Nevertheless, he never forgot the kindness of the monks. The internal organization of the monastery left a deep impression upon the rebel. When Nemanya built his own monastery in Serbia (Studenitsa) some 20 years later, the impact was still vivid; he wanted the *Evergetis Typikon* to be adapted for use in his monastery. Apparently, Sava felt the same way about the right Typikon for Chilandar.

Today's historians claim that whoever undertook to translate and adapt the Evergetis Typikon did a rather inadequate job. They claim that the old Serbian version, as known, was unclear, confounding and amorphous in many instances. The text was fully understood only much later, when a new scholarly translation of the Evergetis Typikon became available.

In his *Chilandar Typikon*, Sava instructed the monks to take Holy Communion three times a week. He maintained that if "a sick person or a man with many wounds avoids telling the doctor about his predicament, he will find it rather difficult to regain his health. The same is true of those who seek to heal their souls; they will encounter even greater difficulties if avoiding Confessions" (Article 7). Sava explained that the monastery consists of two parts: body (monastery) and soul (prayers) (Article 9). Sava instructed his monks "not to take any oil or to drink any wine on Wednesdays and Fridays." As for "Tuesdays and Thursdays we may eat even octopuses," he said. Saturdays and Sundays are usually fish days, while during the Holy Apostles' fasting period (July 1-12, although length of fasting period varies each year depending upon date of Resurrection), Sava recommended drinking wine "with savor, twice a day, because of dry weather and dehydration" (Article 10). For days of strict fast, Sava prescribed "soaked lentils and raw uncooked vegetables. . . and to be merry if fruit happens to be available, or caraway seeds are found in the lean dip." Sava suggested that the novice pay attention to what was being sung in the morning service: "If 'Hallelujah' replaces 'Praise ye the Lord' then rest assured it is a fasting day. . . ."

Article 12 of Sava's *Typikon* starts with following words:

In the name of the One God the Father Almighty I beseech of you to keep this monastery free of all bishops, and the Protos and of other monasteries, as well as of the patriarchs. And let it [the monastery] be under no one's jurisdiction, whether imperial or ecclesiastical, or else, but [under the jurisdiction] of the Most Holy Birth-Giver of God Hodeghetria, of the prayers of our blessed father (Simeon), and of the one who performs the duties of the hegumen in the monastery.

Sava was not impressed by the mere number of monks in the monastery; the quality of the monks was of much greater concern, their moral values and spiritual dedication. "It is always better to have one who does the will of the Lord than a great number of those who do not carry out the law." (Article 25 of the Typikon). "Elderly monks should not keep a " servant'; however, the novice should make a point of obeying the elders, the illiterate should pay attention to what the bookish monk has to say, just as the ignorant should listen to the enlightened one" (Article 26).

In the coenobitic monastery monks eat together in the "trapeza" (refectory) and "no monk should ever prepare his own food in his cell" (Article 29). Monks should not hoard money or other valuables, they should talk in low whispering voices and as little as possible, because "by holding your lips, you come out reasonable and wise." Monks should keep correspondence with relatives and friends to the bare minimum. It goes without saying that no one should ever move or remove relics, sacred vessels, liturgical books, icons, etc., or let go to waste anything that belongs to the monastery.

Article 40 is of special interest because it deals with the "hospital wing" of the monastery. It is generally accepted that the Chilandar hospital was the first by Serbians. The otherwise very rigorous legislator, Sava, showed a soft spot for "our sick brethren." He instructed the hegumen to "set aside a lkellionj which would look like a hospital, with several beds, and would serve the infirm, where the sick can lie down and rest. There ought to be assigned a monk acting as a nurse who would look after them. And if one nurse does not suffice, two of them should be assigned. . . . And the hegumen should frequently, not rarely, visit the sick, see to it that everything is in order, and bring to the brethren whatever they may need. . . ."

Article 42 deals with Sava's kellion in Karyes, which has its own *Typikon*, also written by Sava. Experts point out the difference between the two typika: basically, they reflect two different monastic traditions. The *Chilandar Typikon* belongs to the predominant Mount Athos type of monasticism, based upon rules codified by Theodore the Studite, in the ninth century. The *Karyes Typikon* is different, of the Jerusalemian type, formulated by St. Sabba the Sanctified in the sixth century. Prof. A.E. Tachiaos of Thessaloniki points out that the pronounced difference between the two typika, both written by Sava Nemanjic, indicate that the author consulted a different source in each case. Tachiaos underlines that "Sava was the first Serbian, and, in fact, the first Slav monk of the Holy Mountain, to bring a novelty to the Athonite monastic tradition. . . he restored the direct contact between the Athonite monasticism, the one fostered by Constantinople, and the original source of asceticism, the one of Jerusalem." 1

NOTES

1. A.E. Tachiaos, *Uloga Sv. Save u okviru slovenske knjizevne delatnosti na Svetoj Gori*, Istorija i predanje, p.87, Belgrade 1976.

Chapter V

SAVA'S MAGIC

By virtue of the year of their birth, Serbia and Chilandar were twins. One should never forget that. Born in the same century, children of Nemanya, of the same faith (viz. Serbian Eastern Orthodox) their Serbian blood obviously contributed to their long lasting loyalties. Never did the two separate; they shared the same destiny for eight centuries.

Their oneness started when Nemanya realized there could be no nation, independent and autonomous, without an organized national church, autocephalous and subordinate to no outsider. Nemanya took care of the first part of the premise, national independence; Sava had to shoulder the second task, the religions and ideological autonomy. Throughout the long ordeal of parrying and fending off both Constantinople and Rome, militarily and spiritually, the warrior Nemanya and the educator Sava both had one goal and were of one mind.

By a strange twist of history, when Nemanya, the statesman, assumed the "angelic face," i.e., became monk, Sava, already a monk, had to become a statesman. Thus, the continuity of Serbia's striving suffered no lapses; it was never interrupted. Two national aims, independence and autocephaly, were achieved without a break in continuity.

When Nemanya died (1199), both the homeland and the monastery were in their infancy. In the opening years of the 13th century being fatherless was a calamity. The dawn loomed ominous for the Slavs. Just as they managed to break out of the slavery cycle and receive recognition in the West as part of the Christian world, it appeared as though they might belong to the wrong side of Christendom. In the eyes of some interested parties (such as Venice, Rome, Paris, or Cologne) siding with Constantinople was a heavy liability. This became quite evident when the Dalmatian city of Zara (1202), and the "City of Constantine" (1204) were sacked by those European Christians who profited from the Crusades. In 1208, Sava wrote that he had to abandon the peace and quiet of his "m'lchalnitsa" ("House of Silence") in Karyes, because Serbia, his homeland, was in greater need of him than was his monastery. There is that well known passage from Sava's *Life of St. Simeon* (Nemanya):

> After I spent eight years over there [on Mount Athos], many disorders and rampages began in the area. As the Latins passed through and conquered Constantinople, they took former Greek lands, they spread all the way to us, even raided this holy place in the ensuing chaos. At about that time I received a message from Stephan [the son of Nemanya] and his brother Vukan. Their supplication read: "We are told that nations are in great commotion there [on the Holy Mountain], and our blessed father, Simeon, who was our master and our teacher [still] rests over there. This is why we beg of you not to spurn us, but, in the name of the Lord, please take the venerable remains of our master Simeon and bring them here, so that his blessings may fall upon us as well."[1]

On his death bed, Nemanya had asked Sava to take his body to Studenitsa. He wanted to rest in Serbian ground, in his Church which he built before he renounced his throne. Consequently, when Stephan and Vukan wrote to Sava, they were in fact reminding Sava of their father's wish. "And I, taking his venerable remains, began the journey," writes Sava. He must have been in his mid-thirties when he returned to Serbia after an absence of some 18 years. He left Serbia as a teen age prince and returned as a cleric with the rank of Archimandrite.

On this particular journey, Sava was not simply supervising a funeral cortege; he was to preside over an extremely important national reconciliation mission. For his two brothers were on a divisive course, at each other's throats, which threatened the very survival of the realm that Nemanya had established.

As Sava's somber column reached Serbia, it was met at the border by Stephan and the Bishop of Rascia (Serbia) while the other brother (Vukan) was rushing from Zeta, the coastal area, to meet the procession at Studenitsa. As the column with the dead sovereign approached the monastery, waiting at the gate was Hegumen Dionisije, the very man Nemanya had appointed before departing for the Holy Mountain. Before the second burial of their father Nemanya took place, the two sons "buried their hatchets," embraced each other and let "bygones be bygones." Everybody was happy, and many believed the nation's wounds were healed.

His mission, the reconciliation of the feuding brothers accomplished, Sava prepared to return to Karyes. He had, however, a premonition that his wish would not be granted. The longer he delayed departure, the clearer it became that his involvement in Serbia's affairs would keep him away from the Holy Mountain for some time.

Sava busied himself with the editing of the *Studenitsa Typikon*, and with the laying of the first foundations of the future independent Serbian Church. Once begun, the job seemed endless; it had to be done from scratch. The needed manpower was unavailable, administrative ability nonexistent, there were no liturgy books, and, besides, there were only a few people who were able to read them. Literacy among priests was practically nil. Sava became involved in a task that required work beyond measure and infinite time. Consequently, he decided to build himself another "House of Silence," this time near the Studenitsa Monastery. He was not a man to enjoy living in a palace.

Sava's presence in Serbia had the effect of a tonic; soon, the divided and deeply perturbed nation burst with new energy and hope. The Chilandarian gave the nation a sense of purpose by changing the flow of national energy from destructive to constructive. He recruited many a novice to carry the burden of the national effort that was to come. He enlisted the aid of a number of Chilandar Elders to educate and direct the novices. Thus, Sava set his homeland on a definite course; at least he believed he did. Somehow, the implementation of his idea was temporarily stranded.

There were many roadblocks ahead, hurdles, and obstacles of all kinds. Internally, the anti-clerical heresy of the Bogomils was strong, and widely spread among the Serbians. (Bogomils are defined as members of a heretical Bulgarian sect which rose about the year 1000 and whose main tenet was that God had two sons, Christ and Satan. Bogomilu was a priest who founded the sect.) In addition, serious external threats were lurking on the horizon. Rumblings from Bulgaria, Byzantium, and Latin-occupied Greek lands were ominous. One Bulgarian protege of Stephan, the ferocious Prince Strez, toyed with the idea of changing sides and turning against his Serbian sponsor. At the same time, threatening clouds were gathering North of Serbia, in Hungary. Under the circumstances, the last thing Stephan needed was an armed confrontation with the wild Bulgarian. Stephan then pleaded with Sava to go to Strez's camp and try to "tame the lion." Stephan demanded this of his brother, who had just finished building his quiet retreat!

Thus, the Chilandarian found himself on another peace mission. He went straight into the "hornet's nest," Strez's headquarters at Prosek, a citadel perched high over the Vardar River. There, he found the rebel banqueting and throwing live war prisoners into the fast-moving stream. Sava and Strez, the monk and the lunatic, bargained and bargained, high above the roaring water, for several days. Then, as Sava thought they had reached an impasse, Strez's life was forcibly ended. It is not clear whether he was murdered or committed suicide. In any case, the miraculous removal of the danger was ascribed to "Sava the Wonder-worker."

Upon his return to Serbia, Sava, with his Chilandarians, continued to concentrate on missionary work. In due time, Nemanya's monastery, Studenitsa, became the spiritual capital of Serbia. Sava, however, wanted to go a step further, to establish a clerical center for the country to serve as the See of the future Serbian Archbishop. He had in mind a National Cathedral, where Serbian rulers would be crowned by a Serbian Archbishop. The See was to be built in the heartland of the Serbian realm, on the river Ibar. It was to be designed, built, and decorated by the best architects, masons, and stone cutters one could find in the land or abroad. This is the manner in which the Church of Serbian Kings, Zhicha(near Kraljevo), was conceived.

Stephan, Sava's brother, supported the idea, until he became apprehensive about the reception abroad of Sava's serjeantcies, notably in Hungary, whose King was the titular "King of Hungary and Serbia." This title had been awarded to the Hungarian kings by the Pope. Stephan had asked (c. 1216) Pope Innocent III (1198-1216) if he - the unchallenged Kingmaker of the period - would consider him for the honor of recognition by coronation. Apparently, Stephan's first request (c.1210) for the crown was either rejected or ignored, probably due to the objection of the Hungarian court. Soon after the second request, Pope Innocent III died, and his successor Honorius III (1216-1227) decided to risk the wrath of the Hungarians for the friendship of the Serbs. He sent the crown and his delegate to officiate at the coronation of Stephan (1217).

Sava did not attend the coronation. He had left the country before the Papal legate had arrived, but most of his team remained behind. Some historians assume that Sava left in anger — disappointed and bitter. Others point out that the separation was brotherly and without rancor. Stephan was gracious and extremely generous when he bid his brother good-bye; he attached a cavalry escort to his brother's party.

There is no doubt that both Sava and Stephan understood the importance of the event. Coronation meant international recognition, the enhancement of the status of Serbia, especially in relation to Hungary, Bulgaria, and in the long run, to Byzantium as well. Certainly, it removed the imminent danger of being attacked by the Latin (Papal) coalition, at that time encircling Serbian lands.

However, it was not long before the King of Serbia sent a messenger to the monk of Chilandar, seeking advice and begging for quick action. It seemed as though the pragmatic King could not handle the pressure of the mighty Curia. Stephan informed Sava that Orthodoxy was endangered in Serbia, that "our father Simeon has hidden his face from us. His oil of myrrh has ceased to flow." That was interpreted as a positive sign of Simeon's disapproval of Stephan's policies. Stephan wanted Sava to go to Nicea, to see the Ecumenical Patriarch in exile, as well as the Emperor, temporarily residing there.

Sava replied with a letter detailing his own plan to remedy the situation. The letter was carried by Sava's disciple, Hieromonk Ilarion of Chilandar. When Ilarion returned and Sava read Stephan's reply, he was extremely pleased. Stephan was in full agreement with Sava's plan and promised unlimited support.

Now, Sava knew, his moment of triumph had come. He moved with the cunning of a worldly diplomat. In Nicaea (1219), he presented Serbia's case so convincingly that he made both Emperor Theodore Laskaris ,(1206-1222) and the Patriarch Manuel (1215-1222) feel guilty. Byzantium's unwillingness to give the crown to the Serbian ruler had forced Stephan to look elsewhere, so said Sava. Byzantine internal dynastic rivalry had weakened the Eastern Empire and Orthodoxy, and contributed to the aggressiveness of the Roman Church. Bulgaria already had been lost to Catholicism. Serbia was now besieged. Under the circumstances, what could the Emperor of Byzantium and the Patriarch of Orthodoxy do to remedy the situation?

History will never know whether Sava's presentation was a clever ploy, an attempt at scare tactics, or a mixture of both? The presentation worked; Sava returned to Serbia with the official recognition of limited autocephalous status of the Serbian Church. Not only were they (Emperor and Patriarch) willing to agree to the independent status of the Serbian Archbishopric, but in addition they insisted that Sava be the first Serbian Archbishop. Sava had brought along a number of able Chilandarians to let the Emperor make a suitable choice, but Theodore would not hear of it. He told Sava: "It's you, and only you!. . . And, do not argue!. . ."

Thus Serbia had a situation where one brother was recognized by the West, the other by the East. Could it be that they operated in league while creating an impression of hostility?

The stratagem does smell of conspiracy. Was it not Sava who removed himself from Serbia, so he would not perplex the Papal Legate who brought the crown? And was it not Sava who needed that ceremony of coronation more than Stephan, to serve as a trump card when the time came to face the Byzantine Emperor?

Suddenly, everything fell into place for these two brothers who seemed to disagree at times. When the crusading Hungarian King Andreas (Fifth

Crusade, 1218-22) returned from Egypt and saw what had happened, he was so enraged that he turned his army against Stephan at once. Who else but Sava was sent to pacify the Hungarian. The Chilandarian thus went on his third peace mission. What Andreas and Sava discussed is not recorded in history, but it did cause the enraged Hungarian to cancel his campaign. The national legend has it that, on the day of the parley, it was so hot that neither Tokay wine nor water was potable. Andreas complained about his inept quartermaster who failed to provide ice. After the meeting Sava went to his own tent, prayed and asked for a cooling rain. What Andreas next saw were soldiers with bucketfuls of lumps of ice which they collected in the hailstorm which had appeared suddenly. Serbian children are told many tales such as this about the "wonder-worker Sava."

In his lifetime, Sava had to deal with five patriarchs, four emperors and three kings, not counting the two nephews he placed on the throne of Serbia, yet he never thought of himself as a statesman, a diplomat or a man of international affairs. Always he remained a Chilandarian and an ascetic, although temporarily on assignment to clear up whatever mess the political brinkmanship of the laity had created. To his nation, he became a role model and a style setter. Later, the whole legion of Chilandarians projected the same image.

When Sava returned from Nicaea with an acknowledgment of the independence of the Serbian Church, no one was more shocked than Homatian, the Archbishop of Ohrid. Ecclesiastically, Serbia was under his jurisdiction. He cried "foul play" and he was right. By going directly to the Patriarch, Sava had gone outside the proper channels, circumventing his superior. The Patriarch never should have received Sava without at least informing Homatian, the appointee of this very same Patriarch. Formally, Homatian had a canonically sound case. Politically, his case was hopeless.

First, Homatian was the head of the Bulgarian Archdiocese at the moment in history when the Patriarch had no sympathy for Bulgarians. Second, he was an ally of the Despot of Epirus, Theodore Komnenos, who connived with the Latins, and was the rival of Theodore Laskaris. But Homatian was not a person to give up easily. He corresponded with two patriarchs on this matter, and kept writing to Sava accusing him of usurpation. He called Sava a "simple hermit" who was trying to solve "world problems," who rode "pedigreed thoroughbreds," reveled in "banquets," and who sought the "title and dignity of Archbishop of Serbia!"

Such a portrayal of the Karyes hermit was, of course, rather far-fetched. In fact, Sava's diplomatic style carried one indelible trademark: He may have been required to act as a diplomat, but he never ceased to live like a monk. He never stayed at palaces, but always in monasteries—more to the point, "his own monasteries" , monasteries he had either restored or built, partially if not from the ground up. In all of his numerous monasterial residences he was called "the second Ktytor," if not "the founder." When in Constantinople, he stayed at the Evergetis Monastery. In Thessaloniki it was always the Philocalos Monastery. On Mount Zion, he was more than welcome in the St. John the Forerunner Monastery, which Sava had built for the convenience of Serbian pilgrims. On the Holy Mountain, Sava maintained his base at the Vatopediou Monastery before he moved to Chilandar. In Serbia, he resided in Studenitsa, and later in Zhicha. In Bulgaria, Sava felt at home in the Rila Monastery.

Basically, Sava was a born teacher and an educator, national in scope. A first-class organizer, Sava clearly recognized the distinction between religiosity in general, and the national faith, indigenous and independent. The way he felt, Serbia had to be nonaligned spiritually, as well as politically.

Wherever he went, abroad or within the country, Sava carried books — books in Greek, Hebrew, or Arabic, a few of them in Russian and Serbo-Slavonic; books that would be read, translated, adapted, or plagiarized. The books in the Serbian language, he wanted transcribed, shortened, illuminated, and or used as primers. Thus, returning from Nicea, Sava stopped at the Philocalos Monastery in Thessaloniki. There he made the list of books which he felt to be needed for his organization of an independent national church. He was able to collect most of them in Thessaloniki, the "City of Orthodoxy," where they were brought from other centers of Christianity. They were canonical and liturgical books, or codices of various types. One of those books was the famous *Krmchija* ("Book of Steering"), another was Photios' "*Nomocanon*," as well as Zonara's "*Synopsis*." At the same time, Sava searched among the Greeks for capable and knowledgeable administrators, and for Serbian monks with proficiency in the Greek language, who were needed as translators. It is rather remarkable that Sava, who had such an exceptionally successful visit with the Niceians, was now welcome among the Greeks of Epirus who supposedly were pro-Latin. The Greeks probably envied the good fortunes of Sava, and the independence he had won for Serbia.

Dimitri Homatian, the Archbishop of Ohrid, was not the only churchman of a high rank who was upset by Sava's success. At the other end of Serbia, the Roman Catholic Bishop of Antivari (today Bar),who was the titled "Primas of Serbia," and who had the spiritual jurisdiction over the Roman Catholics in Serbia, was equally dismayed. After Sava had established two new dioceses (eparchies) in the coastal area of Serbia, the Bishop complained to the Pope about an "increase in proselytism." The seats of Sava's new dioceses were in the immediate vicinity: one on the island in the Bay of Kotor (now island Prevlaka), the other in Ston (Dalmatian peninsula Peljeshats). Sava's organizational scheme perturbed Homatian as well, when the Serbs established a new diocese in Prizren, close to Ohrid. Altogether, the new independent Serbian Archbishopric was divided in ten dioceses, with the Zhicha Monastery becoming the See of the Archbishop.

On his way back from Nicaea, Sava asked several capable Chilandarians to return with him. Metodije, the former hegumen of Chilandar, was appointed Bishop of Rascia (central Serbia). Hieromonk Ilarion, another prominent Chilandarian and Sava's collaborator, became Bishop of Zeta. Rascia and Zeta were the two focal regions of Medieval Serbia.

On Ascension Day of 1220, first Serbian Archbishop Sava was installed in Zhicha; he then crowned his brother Stephan "King of All Serbian Lands and Littoral." Thus the King of Serbia, whom history knows as "First-Crowned," just as properly should be called "Twice-Crowned".

Historians still disagree as to whether the second coronation took place at all. If it did, its significance was rather symbolic. It was a way of confirming the independence of the young nation. It was an assertive motion, not a hostile act against the Pope or anyone else. To Sava, the Slav liturgy and Eastern Orthodox tradition, not an alleged hatred of Rome or Latins in general, were decisive factors, writes a Slovenian priest.[2] Latinophobia, in Sava's case, had yet to be proven. Many believed that Sava refused to yield to Roman pressures, which is a far cry from open hostility. "There are numerous data that indicate Serbia's firm resolution not to permit to be drawn into the controversy between Byzantium and Rome."[3]

The controversy has affected Balkan affairs adversely ever since the ninth century, when Bulgaria and Serbia were won over for the East, while the Croats were favored by the West. Later, the two centers of Christianity definitively separated in the 11th century; Rome and Constantinople continued feuding in their common border areas, and the realm of, Medieval Serbia was never free of their contention.

In the 13th century, when Sava insisted upon religious independence from the East, he was in fact, continuing the policy of Serbian Zeta rulers of the 10th and 11th centuries in their dealings with the West. Zeta rulers insisted that the Catholic Archbishopric of Antivari be recognized by the Papal Curia as an "independent clerical organization." Two famous Popes, Gregory VII and Clement III (11th century), confirmed this particular status of the Antivari Archbishopric. Thus, whether dealing with

Roman Catholic or Eastern Orthodox Christianity, Serbian spiritual leaders insisted upon religious autonomy and ecclesiastic independence.

For Sava, the founder of Chilandar and the spiritual leader of the Serbian nation, independence constituted the mainstay of liberty. He wrote this into the *Chilandar Typikon*, "for the monastery to be under no one's jurisdiction, whether imperial or ecclesiastical."

He was fully aware that, wedged between two incompatible Christian societies, the young Serbian nation was susceptible to attack, persuasion, and temptation. Unless guided by stalwart spiritual leaders, the inexperienced nation could not avoid the perils of ensnarement. Those guides had to be exponents of autochthonous national aspirations—the Chilandarians.

NOTES

1. Djordje Trifunovic, *Primeri iz stare srpske knjizevnosti*, (Belgrade 1967), p.4.

2. Franc Grivec, *Sveti Sava i Rim*, p.21.

3. Stanislav Hafner, *Svetosavska crkva i Rim u XIV veku*, Istorija i predanje, (Belgrade 1976), p.384.

Chapter VI

CHILANDARIANS AT THE HELM

Sava was in his early 60's when he died in Trnovo (1236), the capital of Bulgaria. He was enroute to Serbia, returning from his second pilgrimage to Jerusalem. The private journey had an official component, because the Bulgarian Tsar Jovan Asen II (1218 - 1241), and his Patriarch Joachim, had pleaded with Sava to put in a good word with his Byzantine friends to help speed up the official recognition of the Bulgarian Patriarchate. Sava's magic, his tact and diplomatic skills, worked once again, and he arrived in Trnovo with an abundance of good news. The Bulgarians were elated. Since it was the Christmas Season, many church services were held. Sava himself celebrated a few Divine Liturgies between Christmas Day and Epiphany.

In this joyous atmosphere, as Sava prepared to depart, he suddenly became ill and developed a high fever. It proved to be fatal in view of his fragile physical condition, weakened and sapped by lifelong fasting and strict asceticism. To the embarrassment and sorrow of the Bulgars, Sava died while visiting with them. Serbia was in shock when the news of Sava's death in a foreign country reached the homeland. According to Sava's biographer Domentian, the stunned nation was informed of something else as well, i.e., that Sava had always hoped to die abroad and be buried in foreign soil just as his father had been. Presumably, he believed that in this way, he could repeat the wonderworking feat of his late father Nemanya. According to Domentian, Sava's last prayer in Trnovo included the following words: "I worship Thee, I praise Thee, Oh My Lord, for Thou hast fulfilled also my last desire: to die in a foreign land; forgive me my doubts." Sava died on January 14 (Julian calendar).

Prior to going on his second pilgrimage to Jerusalem (1234-35), Sava had given up the Archbishop's throne. He surprised the nation with his choice of successor. Contrary to what the nation expected, i.e., a Chilandarian to succeed him, Sava chose a monk from Zhicha. The choice must have incensed quite a few of his close old-guard collaborators, but Sava did not want an older person to shoulder the burden whose weight was known only to him. The successor was trained for many years in Zhicha under Sava's watchful eye and strict control. Tradition has it that a young man strolled into the monastery one day and expressed a desire to see Sava, his hero. The newcomer stated that he had come all the way from Srem (at that time part of northern Serbia) and that his name was ARSENIJE.

As Archbishop, Arsenije proved to be an excellent choice. Valiantly and deftly he guided the Serbian Church for three decades (1233-1263), primarily attending to Church business and staying out of public affairs. As a villager, he had no taste for pompous sycophants of the court, and his self-effacement probably explains why history failed to be more generous with annotations on the life and work of the second Serbian Archbishop. His time was not an easy one. In the course of three decades, three sons of Stephan the First-Crowned sat on the royal throne. Needless to say, successions were administered with typical medieval unconcern for civility. Since the East-West interplay of political intrigues was going on full blast, the management of religious affairs required a steady hand. Fortunately, not being a political animal, Arsenije succeeded in remaining uninvolved, above complicity and conniving, but respected by all. Serbian Church chroniclers acclaim Arsenije for his positive role in the successful retrieval of Sava's body from Trnovo. Arsenije was the one who moved the See of the Archbishopric (1253) from Zhicha to Pech when Tartar invasions endangered central Serbia. Arsenije was the one who brought Sava's body to the Milesheva Monastery, which was built by Sava's nephew, King Vladislav. Thus Sava had two burials as did his father Nemanya. And both founders of Serbia died abroad, though not in exile.

The Serbian Church has sanctified Arsenije (c. 1273), the cleric of Chilandarian training who never saw Chilandar, but whose character was shaped by the first and the greatest of all Chilandarians.

A century later, Arsenije's cult was widely accepted in Russia. He was buried in Pech, future See of the Serbian archbishops and patriarchs, but his remains had to be moved several times. Not an unusual feat in Serbia, where kings, archbishops and patriarchs (namely their dry bones and skeletons), often had to be moved from one safe place to another. Following one such hurried exit, Arsenije's remains were temporarily lost, only to be found (1920) in the Monastery Zhdrebanik.

The third Archbishop of Medieval Serbia was Sava's namesake, SAVA II (1263-1271). An authentic Chilandarian, he took his monastic vows in this Serbian Lavra. Before being elected hegumen, Sava went on a pilgrimage to Jerusalem, visiting the same places that St. Sava had visited. Not only was St. Sava his hero, but his uncle as well, because Sava II was the youngest son of King Stephan the First-Crowned. Thus the Monastery Chilandar could boast of another monk of royal blood on its roster.

About the middle of the 13th century Sava had been recalled to Serbia. At that time his brother, King Urosh I (1242-1276) needed a trusted person for the sensitive post of Bishop of Hum (in the coastal area). There, Sava served in a double capacity: in addition to being the emissary of Archbishop Arsenije, he was the confidant of his brother, the King. The Bishop was exposed to considerable pressures. On one side, he had to deal with assertive Papal missionaries in the area; on the other, there were those solidly entrenched Bosnian Bogomils.

When Sava became Archbishop of Serbia, he became an even closer collaborator of his brother. King Urosh I was a very rational ruler; he insisted upon national discipline and supremacy of national interest. A national religion, independent of foreign hierarchies, was his credo; while religious denomination, whether Roman Catholic or Eastern Orthodox, seemed of lesser significance to him. After all, his own wife was a Roman Catholic Princess. In the King's opinion, dignitaries of both Churches had to be evaluated primarily in terms of their loyalty to Serbia.

Sava II, being a graduate of what is often called the Chilandarian Spiritual Academy, should have had no qualms with the policy of his lay brother. Thus, when sectarian Venice-supported the Archbishop of Dubrovnik and tried to take away the historical precedence of the Antivari Archbishopric in the Serbian provinces, both Urosh I and Sava II, as heads of secular and ecclesiastical power in the country, responded in unison. They sided with the "independent (Roman Catholic) Archbishopric of Antivari. "

Sava II died in Pech and was buried there. Later he was canonized by the Serbian Church. He was the first of the series of Chilandar hegumens who would ascend to the highest position of the Serbian Church. Out of twelve heads of the Serbian Church, nine (possibly ten) were in one way or another, connected with the most famous alumni in the history of Serbia. Today, fresco portraits of Sava II can be found in four Serbian monasteries (Grachanica, Dechani, Pech and Sopochani).

Who the forth Archbishop of Serbia was remains debatable. Historians disagree on whether the former Chilandar hegumen, Danilo, mentioned most often, really presided over Serbian Church affairs as a precursor of Archbishop Janichije. There are accounts, however that Danilo I was "dismissed" after a "very short time." What is not known is the reason.

There are several theories, all speculative. Most probably, Danilo I could not "stomach" the policy of reconciliation with the West, and he must have resented what he perceived as the increase of Western influence at the Serbian Court. Western queens and their ladies-in-waiting, confessors, German engineers, foreign craftsmen and miners, their households, guests and teachers—living in enclaves yet provoking great curiosity and attention among the Slavs—must have bothered the Chilandarian. Danilo I became a "non-person" of Serbian medieval times—one of several that have been rudely obliterated from the historical records by the silence of biographers and chroniclers. In this particular period, divisive political forces were very much alive in Serbia, and he (Danilo) obviously was regarded as belonging to the "nay" party.

When the new candidate for the position was proposed, King Urosh I made sure he got the man of his choice. JANICHIJE I was not unknown to the King. This Chilandarian was the playmate of Sava II during their younger years, and he remained Sava's loyal friend throughout their monastic period. Janichije I occupied the throne of the Archbishop of Serbia for four years (1272 - 1276), a period not long but extremely tense and critical. Janichije is remembered in the history of Serbia as loyalty epitomized. Being a close friend of Sava II, he could not but be as close to Sava's royal brother. King Urosh and Janichije learned to know each other better after Archbishop Sava II had transferred Janichije from Chilandar to Studenitsa, the "Lavra of St. Simeon." The rapport established at that time seemed to have been decisive when the search for the new Archbishop began. Urosh's candidate was Janichije; the King wanted him and he got him.

Janichije and the King worked very well together. It was not the similarity of views, however, that made them get along but Janichije's boundless loyalty to his King in difficult times. The Archbishop felt that under the circumstances any opposition to the King would be tantamount to national treason. On purely moral grounds, policy aside, Janichije could not agree with the forces of internal opposition which were headed by the King's son, Dragutin. It was a question of propriety and decency not to rise against one's own father, so felt Janichije, especially in view of foreign difficulties.

Janichije must have been horrified by the external situation. This was the time when the Byzantine Emperor, Michael VIII Palaeologos (1259-1282) was confirming the view of Ohrid Archbishop Homatian, denying the canonicity of the Serbian Autocephalous Church. It was the time when the Byzantine Emperor, for reasons of his own, intended to accept religious union with Rome, and had no sympathy for Bulgarian or Serbian independent Orthodoxy. Confronted with such developments, what was the

Serbian King to do? To defy the Emperor of Byzantium and the Pope at the same time? To stand up against the Pope and his mighty Catholic coalition, or oppose the Byzantine Emperor who had kicked the Latins out of Constantinople (1261) and had given rise to subsequent vigorous Byzantine cultural and political renaissance?

King Urosh could see no way out but to accede to the wishes of Rome and Byzantium. As for his Archbishop he clearly saw the danger for Serbia to lose its hard earned religious independence. However, there was no other recourse but to go along with the King's reasoning and to pray. Seldom was a Chilandarian in a tighter spot. How could he agree to deliver the Church of Saint Sava into the hands of the Pope?

The gentle soul, Janichije, must have prayed fervently, because history had spared him the ultimate humiliation; his King Urosh had been deposed by his son Dragutin and interned in a faraway province. The loyal Archbishop immediately self-exiled himself; he went with the King. In the meantime, the assiduously prepared Council of Lyon (1274), which was supposed to tie the wedding knot of a union between the two centers of Christianity, ended in discord. Serbia's plight was not over yet, but at least the nightmare was gone.

For three years the deserted throne of the Serbian Archbishop remained vacant. As long as Janichije I was alive, no Chilandarian dared accept the honor. Neither had the new King (Dragutin 1276-1280) been particularly eager to force the issue and name the successor. The King had plenty of problems of his own without adding this one to his agenda. His poorly managed military campaigns against the Byzantine forces had hardly enhanced his image in the country. In addition, being married to the daughter of the King of Hungary, and conniving with the Latin leader, Charles d'Anjou, did not help his popularity. Dragutin indeed had many reasons to be an unhappy King. Disheartened and despondent, he soon lost the desire to rule and abdicated in favor of his brother Milutin.

Archbishop Janichije died in exile in 1279, one year before the death of King Urosh, who in the meantime had become Monk Simon. Urosh's son Dragutin agreed to have his father buried in Sopochani, Urosh's monastery. Now Serbia witnessed an ironic lesson in tolerance: Urosh's widow Jelena, of Catholic faith (Helen d' Anjou), arranged for Janichije's body to be brought to Sopochani as well. Those two loyal friends in life, she felt, should not remain apart in death.

Queen Jelena acted out of respect and sincere appreciation of Janichije's unwavering loyalty, but her action was remedial in another respect as well. The new Serbian Archbishop JEVSTATIJE I (1279-1286) was now able to re-establish a working rapport with the Serbian Court and also to regain

the influence which the Chilandarians had prior to the crisis. Jevstatije I
was a well known Chilandarian. As a very young monk he was sent from
a Kotor area monastery to Chilandar to attend the "Serbian Spiritual
Academy" where his extraordinary qualities were quickly noticed by
monastery elders. Soon Jevstatije was elected hegumen. Medieval
chronicle's often referred to Hegumen Jevstatije, i.e., when ascertaining
the time frame of an event ("at the time of Hegumen Jevstatije"). Also
they often pointed to his journey to Jerusalem ("before"or "after"
Jevstatije's journey to Jerusalem). Jevstatije was not particularly eager to
take over the administration of Serbia's Church affairs. He even pleaded
with King Dragutin not to drag him into the job. When the King remained
adamant in his request, the Chilandarian obeyed.

Jevstatije's presence in Serbia coincided with one of the most decisive
periods in the history of the nation. The country's situation had improved
considerably, as King Milutin (1282-1321), the energetic brother of
Dragutin, was successfully advancing the cause of Serbia. The new King
had catapulted Serbia into the orbit of dominance in Balkan politics.
Jevstatije was the one who had talked the older brother (King Dragutin)
into abdicating in favor of Milutin. This was a decision of great salutary
effect. It enabled the nation to adopt conciliatory attitudes internally and
to identify with the boldness of the new King, externally. At the same
time it opened new avenues of cooperation between the Serbian Royal
Court and Chilandar.

For seven years, Jevstatije I worked on "making the Church prosperous
in every respect," wrote his biographer (Archbishop Danilo II), "weed-
ing out foreign influences, and preventing the wolf from entering the sheep-
fold." Jevstatije cared for his flock with "unslacking concern," although
he himself was in great need of personal health care. He died in Zhicha,
the first Chilandarian to be buried in the new Church of Kings. A few
years later, he joined the procession of traveling Serbian holy cadavers;
his successor had to move Jevstatije's body to Pech to avoid nomadic
marauders. The Serbian Church canonized Jevstatije sometime before
1329.

Archbishop JAKOV, who succeeded Jevstatije, inherited a solidly
established church. He was a Chilandarian hegumen, already extremely
well-versed in canonical matters, when called upon to shoulder the new
task. He directed Serbian Church affairs out of Zhicha and Pech, the latter being a safer place in turbulent times. In the six years that he served
as Archbishop (1286 -1292), the most incongruous problem he had to deal
with was his unpredictable King (Milutin). The King's "moral values
(personal, familial, or political) seemed to be rather loose; he had many

wives and did not feel obligated to keep a promise. Indecision and sentimentality were not his traits, and although he had built many churches, religion exerted no influence on his views or deeds".[1]

When King Milutin, for reasons of political expediency, decided to marry a Catholic nun, the daughter of the Hungarian King, Archbishop Jakov strongly objected to the marriage. When Milutin ignored the counsel of his Archbishop, Jakov proclaimed the marriage non-canonical and forbade the mention of the queen's name (Elizabeth) in the liturgy. No other Chilandarian had gone that far in opposing the king.

Archbishop Jakov died in Pech and was buried there. The new Serbian Archbishop JEVSTATIJE II (1292-1309) was not a Chilandarian. Maybe Milutin had his fill of Chilandarians! After the strong willed Jevstatije I and the rigid Jakov, the King looked for a more flexible cleric. However, the election of an archbishop was not an exclusive right of the King. Participants at the National "Sabor" (Congress) played a part in this exercise as well. They, not Milutin, prevailed in the election of Jevstatije.

King Milutin kept his new Archbishop Jevstatije II busy. Jevstatije could hardly keep pace with Milutin's conquests of Greek provinces, and the ensuing need to form new dioceses, as well as to staff those existing ones with reliable clerics. In fact, the re-staffing meant replacing Greek priests with Serbian [or Macedonian] priests. As the country was growing in size and population its religious homogeneity and its cultural cohesion suffered. By the same token, while the royal scepter was gaining new subjects and army conscripts, the pastoral staff had to herd several different sheep (Macedonian, Bulgarian and even Greek).

Jevstatije II was the one who had caught the ire of Pope Clement V (1305-1314). In 1307, the Pope had advised all Roman Catholics to boycott Serbia; he had issued a bull to that effect. Dubrovnik, the trading city, made the mistake of following the Pope's edict to the letter. King Milutin, siding with his Archbishop, retaliated immediately, threatening litigation for breach of contract against Dubrovnik. The King acted as the autocrat he believed he was. To give credence to his intention, Milutin sent away his Catholic nun-wife. Stunned, Dubrovnik senators recanted shortly, and Pope Clement V retracted his bull.

Jevstatije II died in Pech and is buried there.

His successor was SAVA III (1309-1316), who apparently was in Milutin's good graces. The King knew Sava when he was Bishop of Prizren. This bishopric had in time become an important stepping stone to the highest clerical position in the country. Sava III was a Chilandarian, although never a hegumen. He belonged to the monastery spiritual elite, held the rank of "confessor", and apparently functioned as a Faculty

member of the "Academy". Sava III and King Milutin struck it off from
the very beginning, and the King mentioned his Archbishop in a number
of royal documents.

Sava III acted as a liaison when, in 1318, two Chilandarians (Hegumen
Nikodim and Karyes's kelliot Theodul) came to King Milutin to solicit
support for St. Sava's Karyes hermitage. There was a fourth Chilandarian
who attended this meeting as well, Milutin's own confessor, Joasaf.

Sava III was known as a talent scout; he was the one who first noticed
the potential of the future Serbian Archbishop, Danilo II, and pointed him
out to King Milutin. The productive cooperation of the two leaders lasted
to the end of Sava's life. He died in Pech, where he is buried.

When NIKODIM(1317-1324), another former Chilandar hegumen, became Archbishop of Serbia, he encountered the already mellowed King,
aged and showing signs of ill health. Nikodim was not young either (he
outlived the king by two or three years). The white-haired King and the
white-bearded monastery elder were models of statesmanship, wisdom and
temperance. Nikodim was able to persuade his now calm and serene friend
that time had come for him to bring his exiled son back to Serbia, (Milutin
had previously ordered his son blinded for being implicated in rebellion).
Nikodim succeeded in "turning the fury of (Milutin's) great rage into
tamed gentleness," the biographer writes.

Contemporary documents show that the King referred to Nikodim as
"my brother". Those were not easy times for the King. The Papal Alliance was still hoping to reconquer Constantinople. The Turkish presence
in the area had become a stark reality of Balkan politics. For three years
Milutin's cavalry roamed from one battlefield to another, supporting
Emperor Andronikos.

Milutin did not hesitate to send the old Chilandarian on sensitive
diplomatic missions. He knew that Nikodim was no stranger in Constantinople. As hegumen of Chilandar he had gone there many times on
monastery business. As early as 1313, the two royal brothers (Dragutin
and Milutin) had asked Nikodim to take a message of utmost confiden-
tiality to Emperor Andronikos II Palaeologos and Patriarch Nifon.
Nikodim was a skilled mediator, and for the services of a successful go-
between he invariably obtained some favor for his monastery. At that
time, Chilandar got two chrysobulls from Andronikos II confirming earlier privileges of the monastery. Normally, the intermediary would not be
forgotten by the other side either, usually trying to outdo the first benefactor. King Milutin was second to none in this respect.

It seems unpardonable that so little is known of Nikodim, a great international personality of his time. But, as is the case of other Chilandarians,

the humbleness of the monk frustrated many historical research efforts and probings at almost every turn. In spite of numerous tracks left by Chilandarians, as testimony of actual good works, little is known of the personalities of those who made the marks. Nikodim must have been an extraordinary human being. He enjoyed the full confidence of two seasoned Serbian Kings (Dragutin and Milutin), as well as of two inexperienced one (Stephan Dechanski and Dushan), of three Byzantine Emperors (Andronikos II, Andronikos III and Michael IX), and of two Patriarchs (Nifon of Constantinople and Athanasios of Jerusalem).

Nikodim was the one who crowned Stephan Dechanski, the most tragic figure among Serbian Kings, as well as Stephan's son Dushan, the mightiest of them. Nikodim was well read, proficient in the Greek language, and versed in literary craft. He contributed to Serbian medieval literature his own translation (1319) of the *Typikon of St. Sava the Sanctified* (of Jerusalem). His own *Karyes Kellion Charter* (1322) contains some scant biographical data about author Nikodim. Any young monastic, desirous of learning and receiving an education could always count on Nikodim for support and encouragement. Most of those young men would end up in monastery scriptoriums; quite a few of them in monasteries Chilandar, Studenitsa and Zhicha. In that sense, Nikodim was continuing the work of the first Serbian Archbishop, St. Sava. Had he been alive, he would have loved to see that.

Nikodim died and was buried in Pech; another Chilandarian who was subsequently canonized. One of the small churches (St. Dimitrije's) within the Pech Cathedral structure was built by Nikodim.

DANILO II (1324-1337), Nikodim's successor, undoubtedly fully deserves his special place among the Chilandarians. He was appointed the hegumen of Chilandar at the express wish of King Milutin. In fact, the King wanted Danilo for archbishop already in 1317. At that time, the Sabor leaned toward Nikodim instead. After Nikodim's death, Danilo was considered for the position automatically. Educated, bold and steadfast, with legendary exploits against the Catalans on his record, he was the hero of the Holy Mountain. Indeed, his entire life story reads like a thriller, replete with history, drama and excitement. Yet, Serbian literati have still to discover him. It is difficult to believe that no one has written an historical novel about this extraordinary Serbian monk.

Danilo is another one in the series of Chilandarians who were by birth groomed for courtiers, but felt better suited for monasticism. He joined the club of Serbian medieval runaways (Sava Nemanjic, Sava II, Janichije, Jevstatije II, Nikodim) when he deserted the Court of King Milutin. One night, while accompanying the King, he slipped away and entered the

Konchul Monastery on the Ibar river. This is where he donned the black rasson. The hegumen of the monastery sent Danilo to Archbishop Jevstatije II, who took him under his wing. Soon after, Danilo was dispatched to Pech, where he was promoted in rank. The next thing he knew was a dreamlike transfer to Chilandar on the Holy Mountain. His travel-order specified the purpose of the transfer, advising him explicitly that he was to become hegumen of Chilandar! This must have taken place in the very beginning of the 14th century (c. 1305), because, as he will write later, "raiding Catalans showed up a short time after my arrival."

The raiders were mercenaries, members of the Grand Company of Catalans, whom Andronikos II Palaeologos had hired to defend him against the Turks. Soon they started to terrorize anyone within the reach of their sword. In order to get rid of the nuisance, Andronikos ordered the company stationed at the Chalkidiki peninsula Kassandra. Enraged, the hot tempered Spaniards vented their anger on the nearby Holy Mountain. Thus, the former Serbian courtier, who just got saddled with administrative duties of the monastery elder, now had to learn the trade of a besieged warrior. For three long years, Danilo mustered his troops, consisting of monks and those who sought refuge in the monastery. It is said that within a few months of the Catalan incursion all but the largest and best-defended monasteries were destroyed, and monks were "slaughtered like lamb."[2] During one lull in operations, Danilo decided to pack up the monastery treasures and, heading the convoy loaded with valuables, went in search of Milutin. He found the King in Skoplje.

Catalans must have learned about Danilo's escapade, because as soon as he returned he was besieged again, this time in Old St. Panteleimonos. The clamoring soldiers of fortune demanded that Danilo be delivered to them alive, probably to use him as hostage, and to blackmail the Chilandarians into opening the gate. Strange as it may seem, for the second time in the rather short history of medieval Serbia, the same wall of St. Panteleimonos's had become the scene of negotiations between the monk on the parapet and the furious soldiers at the base. There he was, hegumen Danilo, standing at the same pyrgos once stood upon by Sava Nemanjic. Two Serbian monks in the same predicament!

Tired of siege warfare and arbitrament of the sword, Danilo passed the hegumen's staff to Nikodim (future Archbishop), and retired in peaceful solitude of the "House of Silence" in Karyes. There, the bookish monk was to devote himself to praying, maybe some writing, but mostly reading.

Danilo should have known better. Very soon he was called back to Serbia. King Milutin had a special job for him. The King had undertaken to build a magnificent monastery of his own (Banjska), to be his burial place.   He appointed Danilo to supervise the project.   As Bishop of Banjska, Danilo was also entrusted with superintendency and guardianship of King's gold reserves and treasures (1313).   A year later, while still Bishop of Banjska, Danilo conducted the burial services for Queen Mother Jelena, in her monastery Brnjatsi.

By this time (1314) Banjska monastery was under roof.   Danilo was bored with custodianship duties, and begged the King to let him return to Karyes.   He had hardly taken to his books there when King Milutin wanted him back in Serbia.   This time, Archbishop Sava III needed Danilo in Pech urgently (1316).   When Danilo arrived, a crisis of even greater urgency required his presence in the coastal area, where the seat of the recently deceased Bishop had to be filled by a person of wisdom, tact and courage. Obediently, the Chilandarian went where his nation needed him.   But he could not stop yearning for Karyes; a Serb in his beloved homeland, yet homesick, nostalgic, and set on returning to the Holy Mountain in Greece! Eventually Danilo got his wish.   Once again, he settled in Karyes and devoted himself to two favorite projects of his: planning a pilgrimage to Jerusalem and preparing an outline of a book on the history of Serbia.

At that time, history as a discipline consisted of biographies, of stories about kings and archbishops.   Serbian historiography, Danilo felt, seemed to have begun and ended with the biographies of Nemanya and Sava. Danilo wanted to fill the existing gap of a hundred and some years, and to set up a pattern for future contributors to the series.

Developments in Serbia, however, dragged Danilo away from his favorite projects.   Serbia was going through a transition period.   King Milutin was about to die, the blinded Stephan Dechanski was to ascend the contested throne, and Archbishop Nikodim was not to last long either — all this required Danilo's presence in Serbia.   For the fourth time, Danilo had to return to his native land.   When the general situation in the country seemed settled, and Danilo was ready to retrace his familiar Mount Athos route, the new King asked him to undertake a couple of diplomatic errands.   Danilo was dispatched to the Bulgarian Tsar Michael Shishman (1233-1330), and to Emperor Andronikos II.   Thus Danilo, the Chilandarian, was now going through one more transformation: he became His Majesty's roving Ambassador, a diplomatic trouble shooter.   This episode over, Danilo was finally free—he thought.   Astride his tired mount, which by now must have known every single pothole along the route, Danilo was slowly becoming an author once more.   By the time he arrived in Karyes, he had his entire book planned (in his head).   Alas, the monk must have forgotten the devil never relents!   Hardly had he unsaddled his horse and taken pen in his hand when the bad news arrived: Archbishop Nikodim had passed away.

Luck seemed to have deserted the would-be author, who was now unanimously elected "Archbishop of all lands Serbian and Littoral" (1324-1338). The author-part of Danilo, however, would not let him forget his literary project. It enticed him finally to get it started, and to make sure it would be continued once he departed. He was a man of action, a born leader, his sights set on the future. Like his friend King Milutin, he was a prolific builder of churches as well. Of some thirty houses of religion built or restored, two are the churches of today's Pech monastery: the Church of Our Lady Hodeghetria and St. Nicholas Church. Danilo's impressive building record had only one flaw: the timing was wrong, because nobody could outbuild King Milutin with a grand total of forty churches on his record.

Of all the Archbishops of Serbia, probably no one possessed Danilo's sense of continuity and interaction between past and future. When he initiated the series of Serbian biographies, seven of which he wrote, he made sure younger authors would write a few more, and hoped the collection would never stop growing. He wanted the series to become an uninterrupted literary process, a historical sequence that would continue as long as the nation lived.

Danilo II was the last of the succession of outstanding Chilandarians on the throne of the Serbian Archbishopric. In view of the multifaceted excellence of the team, it is difficult to say whether he was the most illustrious of the alumni. Undoubtedly, he was the most popular Serb of his times. Infinitely positive and constructive, never degrading or fragmenting anything Serbian, he was a rare phenomenon among Serbs. In 1317, King Milutin had firmly promised the Archbishopric to Danilo. At the National Sabor, Nikodim was elected instead. There was no rancor in Danilo's heart; he continued to be of service to his homeland as heretofore. He was the confidant of Kings, confessor of Queens, man of the world and the solitary hermit of Sava's kellion in Karyes. Resourceful and firmly loyal, steadfast in purpose, he could serve wine in the Eucharist spoon or, if need arose, pour the wine down the searing wall at Catalan arsonists. He did not live long enough to perform the crowning of the first Serbian Tsar in Skoplje, which is unfortunate, because Tsar Dushan's would no doubt have been his best biography.

Danilo II died in Pech, and was canonized by the Serbian Church.

In the time span of some hundred fifty years, from Sava I to Danilo II, the Serbian nation sailed through many turbulent waters. On these passages, the ship captaincy was by Kings, but most of the time the navigator

was a Chilandarian. And while the captain, on occasion, examined cur-
sorily the Latin map, the navigator had his sight on the Eastern Orthodox
compass all the time.

In terms of orientation, does this mean that Medieval Serbia was pro-
Byzantine? Broadly speaking one could say: culturally yes, politically
no. In the medieval period, members of the Serbian ecclesia wielded considerable influence and, being the product of Byzantine Holy Mountain
(which promoted the "Orthodox synthesis"), Byzantium could have influenced the Serbian cultural orientation. Politically, however, Serbian
Athonites had never identified with the pro-Byzantine course of Greek
Athonites. In general, non-Greek nationals on the Holy Mountain, i.e.
residents of Slav or Georgian (Gruziyan) monasteries, rarely agreed with
Greeks. Thus a monk of Chilandar or Iveron could have been worlds
apart from the monk of Vatopediou or Great Lavra of St. Athanasios.

There were other Chilandarians who, although not elected to the post
of Archbishop of Serbia, greatly helped advance the cause of Serbia. In
the annals of 14th century Balkan diplomacy, two of them stand out
prominently. Gervasije, for two decades the sagacious hegumen of Chilandar (1317-1337), and Kalinik, the confessor of Milutin's Queen Simonida.
Both of them spent more time commuting between royal courts than being
in the monastery. The services they rendered to Byzantine Emperors are
reflected in numerous chrysobulls safeguarded in Chilandar. In 1321 only,
a total of eight chrysobulls were issued by two rivals (Andronikos II and
III), attesting to the intricacy of the political climate, the importance of
Chilandarian services and the scope of imperial gratitude. In the beginning, those charters and documents dealt with contributions and favors extended to the monastery, but later included generous personal gifts. The
two monks, Gervasije and Kalinik soon became owners of valuable real
estate, consisting of smaller monasteries and their metochia. Andronikos
II and his grandson Andronikos III, as well as John Palaeologos and John
Kantakuzenos, mighty contenders for power and superiority, all needed
King Milutin's friendship. The road to Milutin's heart led through Chilandar. This explains the total of 95 Greek charters and documents that
Chilandar received in twenty years of Gervasije's hegumenship. These
documents were obvious rewards, compensations for services rendered.
The charters confirmed old privileges, corrected past injustices, extended
new favors, but seldom if ever, divulged the nature of the services that
prompted the rewards. Methodically and painstakingly, historians had to
search for missing links. In many cases, the Chilandar component was
the only point of departure.

Today, as in the past, Chilandar archives serve as a major source of information on Serbo-Byzantine relations in the first half of the 14th century.   Who would have thought that humble medieval monks, who themselves looked to the Heavenly Lord for guidance, advise, and help, would have had so many dealings with earthly sovereigns? Or that in our time, students of Byzantine imperial diplomacy would find the members of the medieval diplomatic corps residing in the Serbian monastery?

NOTES

1. Stanoje Stanojevic, *Nasi vladari*, (Belgrade 1927), p.26.
2. John Julius Norwich, et al, *Mount Athos*, p. 39, New York 1966.

Chapter VII

THE EMPEROR IN RESIDENCE

Emperor Dushan the Mighty (1331-1354) was the most eminent medieval ruler of Serbia, the most dominant figure of the Nemanjic dynasty. Also, he was Chilandar's most illustrious friend. And while Byzantine emperors and Russian tsars were generous benefactors and donors, Dushan was more than that; he was a close relative, on the paternal side. No other emperor in the entire world could ever had been so dear to a Chilandar monk.

The imperial ambitions of Dushan are not the subject of this book, but they need to be mentioned in order to have a better understanding of the functional role the Chilandar Monastery played in the overall political schemes of the Serbian Emperor. Dushan had his sight set on the Byzantine throne as did three Greek pretenders. All four needed the widest possible popular support. Dushan, in that respect had an advantage, considering he had the Serbian public opinion solidly behind him. However, he had yet to win the backing of the Greek public. This did not seem easy to achieve because Greek support was already split three ways among the Greek pretenders. Dushan was particularly interested in the support of the Greek clergy. In Byzantium, the emperor was the head of both the State and the Church. The patriarch of Constantinople was appointed by the emperor, but the appointment had to be approved by the Church hierarchy, i.e. metropolitans and archbishops who resided in the larger cities of the empire and who wielded great political power. Due to the fact that high-ranking church leaders came from monasteries, and that the greatest concentration of monasteries was on the Holy Mountain, understandably emperors made every effort to be well received among the Athonites.

When Dushan took the Greek city of Serres (1345), an important junction on the road to Constantinople, he felt the time had come to win over the Athonites. By the end of that same year (November), Dushan recognized the autonomy of the Holy Mountain in a chrysobull addressed to all Mount Athos monasteries. He ordered that all monastery properties taken by the occupying Serbian forces, be returned to the monks. Moreover, he confirmed their previous tax exemptions, fishing privileges, etc. Consensus was possible because the Athonites themselves were eager to reach some sort of agreement with Dushan, who undoubtedly had become the dominant factor in Balkan politics; Byzantologist George C. Soulis writes: "In their eagerness to make secure their privileges and their properties, many of which have fallen into the hands of the Serbian conquerors, they [Athonites] did not hesitate to recognize their new master and to seek agreement with him, just as they were to do later with the Ottoman Turks."[1]

The monks agreed to mention Dushan's name in the Divine Liturgy, and later sent their Anthonite delegation, headed by the Protos, to Dushan's coronation in Skoplje (April 14, 1346). This was tantamount to recognition by the Greek clergy, although one could argue that the Byzantine Patriarch had never given his official blessing to this expression of loyalty.

Dushan insisted on being the patron and protector of the entire Holy Mountain. Contemporary Karyes documents called Dushan "the ruling Emperor," as well as the "Imperial ktytor and benefactor." The Synodikon of the Great Lavra referred to Dushan as "the father of our entire Holy Mountain, who makes the Mountain stronger, helps it and supports it by word and deed."[2]

Dushan also made a special effort to win the confidence of numerous hesychasts (eremetical order) of the Holy Mountain. He asked for a meeting with Gregory Palamas, the leader of the hesychasts, who happened to be in the area at the time Dushan was there. The talks were unsuccessful, primarily because the hesychasts were already committed to support John Kantakuzenos, while Dushan was allied to Kantakuzenos's rival, John V. Palaeologos.

Nevertheless, Dushan's imperial period and his visit to the Holy Mountain (September 1347 - April 1348), remained a memorable event. Even today, a Serbian visitor to the Great Lavra, St. Panteleimonos, Vatopediou or Esphigmenou Monastery, might hear his host relate that the Serbian Emperor had shared a meal with the monastery brethren at this very same refectory, had kissed the very same icon, and had prayed in the same church. Dushan's love affair with the Holy Mountain is well noted among Western historians, particularly when discussing the Serbian period of Mount Athos. James H. Billington writes in his book *The Icon and the Axe*:

Dushan assumed the titles of Tsar, Autocrat, and Emperor of the Romans; styled himself a successor to Constantine and Justinian and summoned a council to set up a separate Serbian patriarchate. He sought, in brief, to supplant the old Byzantine Empire with a new Slavic - Greek empire. To sustain his claim he leaned heavily on the support of Mount Athos and other monasteries that he had enriched and patronized.[3]

Among the monks, the story goes that Dushan toyed with the idea of building an entire new city at Samaria, a rounded little hill adjacent to the port of Chilandar.[4] Another tale discloses that Dushan rode horseback to the top of Athos, where he planted his imperial flag. Supposedly, this is the one still preserved in Chilandar.

Political ambition and expedience notwithstanding, one may still wonder what made Dushan stay a full six months on Mount Athos, and why he took his wife and child along, in obvious breach of the basic bylaws of the Holy Mountain? Undoubtedly, the main reason, according to Serbian historian Vladimir Corovic and others, was the threat of the plague raging throughout Europe at that time. It seems that no historian, American or Serbian, has credited Dushan with a genuine attachment to the Holy Mountain. Today, however, when a Chilandar monk points to the gnarled trunk of "Dushan's olive tree," his heartbeat quickens as he tells you that Dushan took intense delight in talking to the monks. "He sat there for hours. . .." And why not? Was he not in his ancestral home, visiting his own folks? Were not Chilandar and its dependency (Sava's kellion) in Karyes built by "our parent and enlightener, our Master Sava," as Dushan is quoted to have said. In a sense, was not this encounter with the monks some sort of a family reunion?

There is no doubt that Dushan must have been happy and relaxed in the company of the monks. His imperial worries could not have deserted him, of course, but how could he be indifferent to the captivating Holy Mountain legends? How could he resist those imaginative storytellers, whose beliefs and loyalties had no end? Perhaps he secretly hoped, that one day they would include him and his visit into the endless skein of their legends.

Humbly and unassumingly, Dushan visited with "our elderly brother Arsenije, conversing with him at length and delighting in his soul-healing words. . . this honorable and Christ-loving Tsar of ours, Stephan, held Arsenije in high esteem, liked him very much because of his numerous virtues, and he listened to him very attentively," reported one biographer.[5]

In the course of one such conversation, the Chilandar elder, Arsenije, pointed to his spiritual son, Hieromonk Isaija. Then praising him and his qualities, the hegumen said to the Tsar: "One day have him in my

place. . . ." According to Isaija's biographer ". . . ever since, the
venerable Tsar Stephan Dushan has shown such confidence and care,
respect, and homage for our blessed Father Isaija, that I find it beyond
my ability to express it in words." [6]

Once in a while, the intimate trio, Dushan the Tsar, his former confessor
Arsenije, and Empress Jelena, would venture down memory lane. It had
been ten years — the three of them remembered it so vividly — since little Urosh was born. "This happy event and God's blessing was written
into the book of birth by the now Chilandar hegumen, Arsenije, at
Svrachin." Svrachin was Dushan's royal court at Kosovo.[7]

Sessions such as this one must have been deeply moving. Finally, the
time came for two good friends, Hegumen Arsenije, weak as a swaying
candle flame, and Tsar Dushan, the conqueror in his prime, to take leave
of each other. Did anyone of those present have a foreboding of what was
to come? All those wise monastery elders, looking at the fragile son of
the Emperor, had they not a premonition that this boy was to be the last
offspring of the dynasty that gave them the monastery? And the Emperor,
who had reached for his roots and had talked to his forefathers on the
walls, did he sense that he would never enter Constantinople?

Soon after Dushan left the monastery (April 1348), Hegumen Arsenije
". . . walked out of life and into the hands of the good Lord." Soon there-
after, all manner of mishaps and a horrible fate were to befall Serbia: the
sudden death of the Emperor (1355), the ominous defeat at Maritsa River
(1371), the tragedy of Kosovo (1389). Finally, Serbia's disappearance
from the scene in 1459 left Chilandar an orphan.

Ironically, Serbia's hard lot had much to do with Dushan's political gran-
domania. As always, in such situations, ambitious schemes are great as
long as they work out, but catastrophic when they do not. Signs of trouble
began showing even in Dushan's lifetime. Once he had left the scene,
they snowballed.

In order to enter Constantinople, Dushan needed the support of the West.
He needed the blessing of Pope Innocent VI, the leader of the western alliance. In order to do that, the Pope would have had to step on the toes
of many western leaders, something he was not willing to do. Dushan
thought he could induce the Pope to do so by offering to recognize the
primacy of the Curia. He also sent his delegate to the French court to
find a French princess as a spouse for his son Urosh (c. 1354). Both
schemes turned out to be unrealistic and transparent. In the end Dushan
was left to cope alone with the situation in Byzantium, where John Kantakuzenos and his supporters were gaining an upper hand. None of this

augured well, but as long as Dushan the Mighty was alive, it did not seem to matter much.

In addition to foreign policy difficulties, Dushan had created an internal problem, one that stemmed from his 1346 decision to institute the independent Serbian Patriarchate. Defying the authority of the Patriarch in Constantinople, he then named his own Logothete to be the first Serbian Patriarch (Joanikije), who in turn obligingly performed Dushan's coronation ceremony. (Logothete is defined as a Chancellor or keeper of the seal.) The Ecumenical Patriarch responded by proclaiming an anathema — official excommunication of Dushan's Church and, in a sense, banishment of the Serbian nation. This did not sit well with many a Serb, but as long as national security remained unaffected, the anathema was not a subject of public debate. When Dushan died, and his son Urosh ("The Weakling") succeeded him, and when Serbian affairs took a plunge, the clamor of those who wanted reconciliation with the Ecumenical Patriarch became louder. The task of effecting the reconciliation fell upon the Chilandarians. As always, when in need of contact with Constantinople, the nation used the Chilandar connection.

For Dushan, it was easy to make a portentous error on the spur of the moment. For the Serbian Patriarch Sava IV (1354-1375), who succeeded Dushan's Patriarch Joanikije, correcting the damage took some twenty years.

Sava had met Dushan for the first time in 1347, when the emperor visited Chilandar. There Sava was about to replace the aged hegumen. Later in 1354, Sava was summoned by the Emperor and Patriarch Joanikije to Serbia. They met at Mount Rudnik, where Dushan was campaigning against the Hungarians. As the three of them sat in conference, and discussed Dushan's western scheme, the Patriarch became ill and hegumen Sava learned that he was about to become the next Patriarch of Serbia.

By the beginning of the 1360s, the Turks had already occupied the largest part of Thrace. They had taken the cities of Dimotika (1361), Jedrene (1362), and Plovdiv (1363). Looking for help, the government of John V. Palaeologos turned to the ruler of the Serres Region, the Serbian Despot Ugljesha, who himself was in great need of support. Ugljesha was the loudest voice among those criticizing Dushan's ambitions. "He [Dushan] elevated himself to the rank of some celestial judge," wrote Ugljesha to other Serbian grandees, and to Kalist, the Ecumenical Patriarch. With the Turks hot on his trail, Ugljesha wanted a prompt unraveling of the anathema issue, the one that stood in the way of a closer bond with Constantinople.

At the same time, the Ecumenical Patriarch could not have felt at ease with all those Turks milling around. Thus, as soon as it became possible, on his own initiative, Kalist took the first step toward reconciliation with the Serbian Church and nation. In the Spring of 1364, he set off on a journey to the city of Serres, for talks with Dushan's widow Jelena, now nun Jelisaveta in a nearby convent. The only woman who ever visited with the Chilandarians, wife of the Emperor who had caused the break, praised Kalist's initiative, and pledged to attempt to mend the fences between two weakened nations. If the road to reconciliation between Byzantium and Serbia had to go through Chilandar, she was the ideal contact. Indeed this was a rare moment in the history of the Balkans. Two prominent Serbian leaders, Despot Ugljesha and his brother King Vukashin, the former Empress Jelena, and the Ecumenical Patriarch (undoubtedly supported by his Byzantine Emperor) were concentrating on the task of creating a united Serbo-Byzantine front against the Turkish onslaught.

Kalist's ill-fated mission was interrupted suddenly when he died in Serres. There he was buried by Serbian clergy - - the clergy whose Church he had anathematized.

The peace initiative was later picked up by the Serbian ruler, Prince Lazar (1372-1389). He and the Serbian Patriarch, Sava IV, decided to make a fresh attempt, following the martyrdom of Ugljesha and Vukashin (September 27, 1371) at Maritza River and the death of Tsar Urosh (December 4, 1371). A delegation of Chilandarians was formed to take Serbia's reconciliation proposal to Constantinople. The head of the delegation was the former young protege of Dushan, Isaija, now an elder in the monastery. Others were Hieromonks Silvester and Niphon, as well as the Monk Nikola ("the Greek" attached to the group as an interpreter). Out of courtesy, the Holy Mountain Protos, Theophanos, was included in the delegation. On the way to Constantinople, the delegates took time to visit with their imperial friend (Jelisaveta) in the convent near Serres. It must have been a very sad reunion, the saddest possible. . . orphaned Serbian monks being consoled by the widowed Serbian Empress.

In Constantinople, the new Ecumenical Patriarch, Philotei, received the Chilandarians warmly. At the same time, however he seemed to be somewhat apprehensive, even distrustful. One could never be sure about the Serbs. . . . These conferees of his, were they men of the past or of the future? What if they bounce back and get ahead of the Greeks again? Philotei insisted upon one safety clause being written into the reconciliation document; i.e., in case the Serbs, by some miracle, succeed in stopping the Turks and reconquer the Greek lands, never again would they be allowed to replace the high Greek clergy with Serbian clergy. Despondent Chilandarians must have found the request in bad taste; but they had no other recourse than to agree. When they parted, Patriarch Philotei asked the Serbian delegates to deliver his most sincere wishes to Patriarch Sava IV, and he selected two low ranking Greek monks to attend the ceremony of reconciliation in Prizren. At, of all places, the grave of the anathematized Serbian Emperor Dushan, in his Monastery of Holy Archangels.

While Philotei's delegates took their time in arriving, Patriarch Sava IV died (April 29, 1375). Another Chilandarian had burned out while serving his homeland. The previous year, Jelisaveta, the Empress nun had passed away. Ironically, of the three main protagonists of the reconciliation (Kalist, Sava IV and Jelisaveta), not one was alive to attend the ceremony in Prizren. In fact, the whole episode, as far as the Greeks were concerned, sank into oblivion. No Greek source ever registered the fact that Sava IV had been recognized by the Ecumenical Patriarch Philotei in 1375.

NOTES

1. George Christos Soulis, *Tsar Stephen Dushan and Mount Athos*, Harward Slavic Studies 2, 1954, p.126.

2. Dragutin Atanasijevic, *Srpski arhiv Lavre Atonske*, Spomenik 56(SKA), (Belgrade 1907), p.56.

3. James H. Billington, *The Icon and The Axe*, (New York 1966), p.56.

4. Gerasimos Smirnakes, *To Agion Oros*, (Athens 1903), p.485.

5. Mosin, N.- Purkovic, M., *Hilandarski igumani Srednjeg veka*, (Skoplje 40), p.56.

6. ibid., p.64.

7. ibid., p.62.

Chapter VIII

CHILANDAR LITERATI

Serbian medieval literature features qualities of explicit selfhood and distinctiveness, owing mainly to the inner equilibrium, personal and moral, of its creators. Predominantly, Serbian medieval authors were either Chilandarians or Chilandar-educated. The sum of their products attests convincingly to the continued affirmation of Serbian cultural identity.

It is not firmly established who was the first Chilandar author. At the turn of the 12th century, after Nemanya's death (probably at the time of the transfer of his remains to Serbia), an unknown author in the monastery deemed it appropriate to write *The Record of the Death of St. Simeon.* Nemanya himself had left few biographical notes in his *Founding Charter of Chilandar* (c. 1199). His son, King Stephan the First Crowned, the "second ktytor" of the monastery, wrote his own *Chilandar Charter* (c. 1200), which he authored in Serbia. In any case, these three documents are broadly accepted as constituting the beginnings of Chilandar's literary tradition. The lengthy introduction — some 1500 words — of King Stephan's account tells us about his father Nemanya who has " restored the land of his ancestors, and made this nation strong by virtue of his wisdom. . . ." About Nemanya who had abandoned

all the glory and honors of the secular world, which he considered to be worth nothing. . . and who with haste had descended from this highland [Rascia] to reach that plane meadow which is the Holy Mountain.. there to find his sweet-voiced bird, Sava the monk, the great solace of this Christ-loving old man. . . In this holy meadow he [Nemanya] discovered the monastery called Mileie, razed to the ground and totally destroyed. Unsparing of his own old age, he also felt that I, who is not worthy of being called his son, should get involved into the restoration of this holy place. I made his wish come true regarding the church and everything else he wanted me to bring to completion. . . I was

deigned worthy of acting as second ktytor along with him, and to provide for
the monastery, thus, I gave....[1]

Later (c.1216), King Stephan resumed writing about his father once
again. In his version of *The Life of Saint Simeon*, Stephan concentrated
on Nemanya the statesman, not Nemanya the monk. One could not have
expected a king to write from the clerical point of view. The fifty page
text encompassed Nemanya's entire life. The text was written by a son
who respected his father for leadership qualities, courage, and perseverance in fighting Byzantium, who never lost sight of the ultimate aim:
the creation of an independent nation.
    It took a Chilandarian, Sava, to focus on the spiritual side of Nemanya.
Sava wrote about his father on three occasions, in all instances while on
Serbian soil. In two liturgical pieces called *Observances for St. Simeon*,
as well as in the *Studenitsa Typikon*, Sava the author is Sava the monk.
The lengthy introduction to the *Typikon* is in fact what is know as *The Life
of Master Simeon* (written c. 1208). The literacy and sophistication of
both royal sons are impressive. However, Sava's delicate touch and
tenderness make him a more talented author. Congenial, direct and warm,
less formal than his brother and often quite casual, Sava addresses the
reader in the following manner: "Let me tell you about this blessed father
of ours and our ktytor, Master Simeon, from the day of his birth to his
death. . . ." Stephan was not that frank with the reader. The King wrote
for the national hierarchy, whereas Sava had in mind a different audience
in many respects. He wrote for those silent monks in the monastery refectory to whom the biography will be read as often as possible.
    Sava narrates how "everything was extraordinary with this man," he
was "baptized twice, he received the angelic face two times, once with
the Little Schema and then again with the Great Schema, and finally he
had two burials." Exercising special care not to fall into "multiplication"
(Sava's term for copious and bulky writing), Sava crowded four scores of
years into four lines. "It was 46 years since [Nemanya's] birth, when he
received the regency which he held for 37 years, followed by his acceptance of the angelic face, in which he lived another three years. Thus his
whole life amounted to 86 years."
    The words Nemanya spoke when addressing his lords on the day he
gave up the throne read as if they were written at Stratford-on-Avon 35
years later: " ... and now let me leave the throne... short is the path we
travel on this earth, and our life is nothing but smoke, vapor, dirt, and
dust. Life appears for a short while, quickly to vanish, proving that all,

indeed, was only vanity." In the Chilandar death scene, with authentic Hamlet-like quality and sound, Sava soliloquizes: "... There lies the man once feared by so many, who made foreign nations tremble, now looking like one of those foreigners, wrapped in his rasson, laid on the ground, on the straw mat, a stone under his head, humble and servile, ingratiating himself to those around him, begging for benediction and pardon of sins. . . . " When Nemanya finally "fell asleep in Our Lord," Sava fell over his father's face and admittedly "cried in despair for many hours." [2]

What Sava and his brother, King Stephan, wrote about their father was later categorized as literature, but what the two authors had in mind were not purely literary creations. They were driven by a desire to give impetus to the national cult their father wished to establish. They both felt such a cult was necessary and they reinforced it as much as they could. Many Serbs felt that way in those days. What the two brothers started never ceased. New heros were placed on the roster, Sava himself an inevitable first choice of several authors to follow.

After Sava's sudden death in Trnovo, the Chilandar elder, Domentian, wrote *The Life of Saint Sava* (c. 1253). Hieromonk Domentian started his monastic life in Sava's monastery Zhicha. Undoubtedly an exemplary monk, he was subsequently sent to join Sava in Chilandar. There Sava asked Domentian to accompany him on his second pilgrimage to Jerusalem. King Urosh I also must have held Domentian in high esteem, because he commissioned Domentian to write Sava's biography. The same Domentian was later to write again, and in the same genre: *The Life of St. Simeon* (c. 1264).

An erudite theologian and a learned author, Domentian wrote for a learned readership, i.e. people surrounding the King and his court. However, his style was not that one of a hagiographer, and his usage of biblical quotations was relatively moderate. At moments he would turn poetic; his presentations would become most imaginative, and seldom would one find an author with such a remarkable sense of drama. When Domentian ghost-writes the desperate letter that allegedly King Stephan the First-Crowned sent to Sava, the letter read as if the Horsemen of the Apocalypse had galloped through the land:

> After you, the Venerable and Saintly one, left us, our country was defiled by our sins and was afflicted by bloodshed. We became the prey of foreign peoples. Our enemies ridiculed us and our neighbors mocked us because of our transgressions. When foreigners came, they indeed devastated the homeland of the Saint [Simeon], and what the Venerable had gathered in one place they split

asunder as their prey. Some [people] were cut down by weapons, others were taken prisoners. Some were deprived of all their belongings and thereby exposed to utter poverty. And later, when by the help of God those [foreigners] were defeated and had left, another foreigner came - one named hunger, worse than those who preceded him. He took his prey, larger than the one taken previously, and he had no pity whatsoever on our people; he killed without arrows, pierced without spears, cut without swords, murdered without clubs; and he pursued although he had no legs, he grabbed although he had no arms, he stabbed without knives, moved about unarmed yet sowed many corpses, in accordance with the sacred Old Testament, where it is said that when the hand of the Lord killed the first born sons in Egypt, in revenge for His first born Israel, there was no home in all Egypt where there was no mourning and no dead. In the same manner, because of our sins, our whole country was crowded with the dead; they filled the yards, the houses, the roads and the paths. And because of our sins, the grave diggers were unable to bury them but somehow laid them down in the holes dug to store wheat.[3]

By medieval literary standards, Domentian's biography of St. Sava was a lengthy work, some 200 pages. *The Life of St. Simeon*, Domentian's second biography, was much shorter, although also written at the express desire of King Urosh I. At that time the Archbishop of Serbia was King Urosh's brother, Sava II. It is possible they both wanted the biography of their father to be written by the most famous biographer of their time.

Domentian worked in solitary places. The biography of Saint Sava, he wrote in Karyes in the kellion built by Saint Sava. The biography of St. Simeon, he wrote in the peaceful surroundings of a fortified chapel near Chilandar, where he met a talented novice who helped him. The young man was known as "Theodore Grammatikos," which indicated his skill in penmanship. A virtuous teenager, nicknamed "smooth-cheeked," he was of humble origin; his parents hoped someone would notice the talent of their son and help him to break away from the stiff bondage of the medieval tiered social system. The experienced Domentian quickly noticed the potential of the novice—his literary ability and artistic sense that went beyond the limits of a deft monastery scribe. He took Theodore under his wing, and as his "spiritual father" probably hoped to make him into another Domentian. Theodore, who later become Teodosije, proved to be made of non-malleable iron. In style and temperament, the two authors were as remote as possible. Yet they had one thing in common: their passion for writing.

If Domentian had hoped to foster another theologian and apologist, it was not to be. But if he had planned to help a fledgling, he could not have chosen one with greater prospects. By age they belonged to two generations, by literary style they were products of two schools, by social origin they hailed from different worlds. None of these differences, however, affected their cooperation. The young partner possessed a natural democratic bent which prevented him from adopting the cumbersome literary manner of his contemporaries. The older man did not mind this at all. He was satisfied to dictate to his assistant in his way, and let the young talent transpose his expounding into modern usage. The two kindred souls began their first literary project at the Transfiguration Pyrgos, near Chilandar Monastery. Domentian asked the novice to transcribe John Exarch's *Hexaemeron* (Shestodnev). This must have taken place in 1263, because Theodore was forced to leave the Holy Mountain temporarily on account of his young age, and to finish the project alone, at the nearest "methoch" of Chilandar and in Thessaloniki.

Exiled by no less an authority than the Protos himself, Theodore returned to the Holy Mountain as soon as the legal age limit permitted, which was in the year 1264. The next year represented a real breakthrough in the life of the ambitious young man. Theodore Grammatikos became Teodosije the monk by taking his monastic vows in Chilandar. Also, his spiritual father Domentian offered Teodosije the opportunity to test his own writing abilities. Domentian decided to help his young disciple write the biography of no less an eminent personage than St. Sava. Teodosije did not wait to be asked twice; he proceeded with the project immediately. The result was the essay that he titled: "*The Life of St. Sava*, as told by the venerable Domentian, the presbyter of Chilandar, and written by Teodosije, monk of the same monastery."

Historians still marvel at the modesty and the self-effacement of the author who wrote a masterpiece, a truly original artistic piece of work. But Teodosije would not have it any other way. Although he could neither talk nor write in Domentian's manner, Teodosije would never be one to claim authorship of the story "told" by someone else. Besides, the young monk could not have expressed his gratitude to the aged tutor in a more meaningful way.

In the centuries to come, numerous scribes who were asked painstakingly and heedfully to transcribe Sava's "vitae," opted for Teodosije's version. They chose Teodosije over Domentian in the ratio of 3:1, though cautious historians seemed to be more impressed with the older theologian. In fact, it was not an easy choice to make; Teodosije's style was less flowery, unadorned and rather homespun. Teodosije's biography was copied in full or in abbreviated form in over 60 versions, and probably more, since it was copied by Bulgarian and Russian scribes repeatedly.

The historical episode when Stephan wrote his famous letter to Sava, pleading with his brother to come to Serbia and bring along Nemanya's body, in Teodosije's version reads as follows:

> I would like to tell you about the hatred between two brothers [Stephan and Vukan], but filled with shame I hesitate. During this time of hatred and persecution the Serbian land was overtaken by great scarcity and distress... The devil, the sower of discord and hating goodness from times immemorial, reaped a bountiful harvest. Christ-loving brother, Stephan, wrote to his brother Sava, the one who carried God in his heart, in pleading words: "Oh, master and holy father, dear to my heart and my soul, hear the voice of my lament, take heed of my sighs and do not disdain my request. Do us a favor by sending us the myrrh-flowing remains of our holy and venerable father. Have pity on us and bring over here [the remains] yourself, so that with the help of your blessed prayers our homeland would be strengthened. Since you have left us... foreigners have conquered us, our foes have disgraced us, and in our mutual hatred we have become a subject of scoff and scorn, and a spectacle of contempt. Your holy prayers and your arrival, we believe, would bring God's compassion upon us, unite us and help destroy our enemies.[4]

Of the two, Domentian had considerable verve, imagination, and could even sound poetic when he elected to avoid high-sounding rhetoric. But Teodosije was warmer, closer to the people and more convincing. Domentian catered to the national elite, Teodosije was the darling of the humble people, of those who preferred genuine spontaneity to the sophistry of scriptural mysticism. When asked to write *The Life of Peter of Korisha*, a hermit who lived near Prizren, Teodosije went to Serbia, visited the district where Peter lived and researched the subject thoroughly. "The work he subsequently wrote was an outstanding poetic narrative of a dramatic story."[5] Teodosije had no advantage of age or of accumulated experience. But his great asset was his literary integrity. As well as his devotion. He was devoted to his "venerable presbyter," to his modest origin and, most of all, to his fellow-monks. A man of great compassion, he wrote about anchorites living in makeshift huts, in caves and austere cliff-dwellings on Mount Athos. One can sense his heart pouring out for them in these words:

> ...lodged on high mountains which they shared with deer, they had the open sky for a church; their scanty huts, in which they endured were grass bedecked; the sound of bird wings and voices were their only worldly messages... sated with the plenitude of fresh and fragrant air they felt richer than the

richest... others [living] in rocky abysses and gaping ravines, or on the cliffs above the sea, nested like birds, by rain and wind tormented, by sweat and sun scorched, and by cold and frost bone-chilled, there was not a thing that robbers would care to take away from them.[6]

A sublime author who obviously delighted in writing, Teodosije is close even to contemporary readers, and his genuine warmth draws one to him at the very outset. As an author he bares his soul and he cannot help but turn poetic when writing about nature and men in interaction.

A contemporary of King Milutin, Teodosije too had to go on various errands, to represent his King and to attend to national affairs. At such periods, authorship had to be put aside temporarily. Several charters issued by Milutin mention Teodosije in various capacities. Milutin's son King Stephan Dechanski asked Teodosije to be his personal confessor. It is difficult to visualize the former scribe of the Transfiguration Pyrgos among the courtiers, but Teodosije's humble parents, had they been alive, would have been happy. And no doubt the Elder Domentian would have been proud of his smooth-cheeked disciple.

As aged and weariness set in, Teodosije expressed a desire to return to the Holy Mountain. King Stephan Dechanski graciously permitted him to go, and he made sure that Teodosije would spend his days undisturbed— and with a good supply of ink. The royal letter instructed the pro-hegumen of Chilandar to appoint Teodosije for life as Elder of St. Basil's small monastery, often referred to as the "Pyrgos on the sea." There, at the promontory, where two identical oval beaches touch, and the air is fresh and fragrant, Teodosije felt "richer than the richest." Respected as author and monk, he savored the beauty and stillness of nature that surrounded him and his little monastery. "The extraordinary view of the sea horizon offered a well deserved opportunity to relax and rest, after decades of continuous work," writes Professor Djordje Sp. Radojicic.[7] Teodosije died in 1327, at the age of 82.

As we continue the survey of the literary output of Chilandarians, we meet the multi-talented alumnus, Archbishop Danilo II. An outstanding author himself, he also encouraged others to "take up the pen" and help the nation preserve its heritage. He believed in a collective effort, and had dreamed-up a literary project, national in scope. A man of grand design and a visionary, he perceived literature as a joint endeavour - - not one burst, but continuous fireworks, the history of the nation expounded by a sequence of biographers. He called his project *The Lives of Serbian Kings and Archbishops*. He wrote the biographies of three kings, one

queen and three archbishops for the series. His pupils added the rest, for
a total of twenty one "vitae" of prominent national figures. Biographies
of Nemanya and Sava were not included because four earlier biographers
had already written of Nemanya, two of Sava.

The Founding Fathers of the nation were well known to Danilo's generation. He felt it was time to write about those who followed in the steps
of Nemanya and Sava, and of whom Danilo knew so much. To some of
them he was a personal friend, advisor, or confidant. Only Danilo could
be considered a trusted friend by both of the two feuding royal brothers
(Dragutin and Milutin) and survive as friend of father and son in mortal
collision (Milutin and Stephan Dechanski), and only he could have the
confidence of two Roman Catholic ladies (Catheline and Helen), married
to Orthodox Kings. It appeared there was no decision of national significance in which Danilo had not participated, no event of major importance without his presence, and certainly no royal death without Danilo
performing the burial rites. Who else could have written with deeper insight about contemporaries?

Danilo II was the first medieval Serbian author to write about a woman,
Queen Mother Helen,(nee d'Anjou) whose two sons, Dragutin and Milutin,
he knew so well. This is something to marvel about, in view of the attitude of the Serbian clergy toward Roman Catholics at that time. Danilo
liked this "wise" stranger, her "sorrowful eyes," "sweet-speaking lips,"
and her "face of God's angel, radiating like dawn's beautiful rays of many
bright colors." Famous is Danilo's description of the last days of this
"blessed lady of ours who was the protectress of those eminent and those
poor, of travellers and of the lame, as well as of the blind. . . ." Danilo
relates how he rushed to her deathbed: ". . . as soon as I heard about the
imminence of her death, I hastened as fast as my strength would permit."
He tells the reader: "All of us in attendance, when we realized she was
about to pass away, cried and sobbed,' Oh, our Lady and Mother, we see
you quite ready to depart'. . . ." This scene took place at the Queen's
famous palace of Brnjatsi where people from all over Serbia gathered; the
Queen was buried with splendid glory in her monastery Gradats. Attending the burial, her son Milutin wept and cried incessantly, pulling the hair
from his head and flinging himself over the body of his God-loving Mother
". . .[while] all those present, both the humble and the proud, burst into
thunderous crying and sobbing. . .[so much so] that even the ground, at
the sight of the crying King, started swelling and the insensitive stone even
began to crumble. . . ."

It hardly sounds believable that this weeping King [Milutin] is the same
one whom Danilo, in writing his biography, would call "my honorable

and Christ-loving master, the most august, mighty autocratic King. . . ."
According to Danilo, "emperors with majestic names feared him, loved
him and honored him," and "many mighty ones were his subordinates,
because the Almighty Lord, the Emperor of the Universe, liked him as
well." Danilo was clearly his admirer; his King Milutin was described in
one exclamatory sentence: "You are greater than all mighty emperors
taken together, my glorious King!" This glorifying impetus of Danilo's
writings had its purpose, of course, because Danilo was dealing with the
earthly autocrat, not with celestial saints, like the previous authors Domentian and Teodosije. Danilo's hero had to be a hardened, strong person, a
fierce and roaring king, tougher than the invading Tartars who attempted
to raid Serbia. They all drowned in the Drim River, and their leader
Tchrnoglav was beheaded. His head "was fixed on a long lance and
brought to Milutin as an offering," writes Danilo.

One wonders whether it was due to astral influences that Danilo seemed
never to have been able to concentrate on what his position called for. As
the Hegumen of Chilandar, he was a warrior; as Bishop of Banjska, a custodian of gold treasures; as Archbishop of Serbia, exhaustively thinking
of literature; as a cleric, unable to extricate himself from secular affairs
and diplomacy. Yet, this strange tale of his must have helped him enormously at the time of authorship. Of all the earlier authors, not one had
the reportorial skills of Danilo, who wrote as a witness would. He knew
the place, the date, the day of the week, those who were present and who
had participated in the event, as well as what was said by whom. All this
was invaluable to historians who would later try to recreate the event.

Chilandar was home to numerous other men of letters who, though not
authors in their own right, amply deserve to be mentioned. They belonged
to that steady and reliable, mostly anonymous, breed that seldom emerged
from their sunless working quarters; only their works saw the full light of
day. The monastery scriptorum was their whole world.

The life of a medieval scribe, in general, was not an easy one. Those
laboring in larger monasteries may have had more favorable working con-
ditions, but their task required inexorable concentration and tireless attention. On occasion, human frailty would gain the upper hand, and the
scribe would leave one of those unforgettable marginal notes that are the
delight of historians.. short, concise notes that tell so much about the human
side of those stolid medieval Xerox machines. One of them would con-
fide to the reader: "... to tell you the truth, I wrote this in freezing cold,
and what's more the ink was bad." Another would explain "Too old am
I for this, I wrote with glassy eyes." Still another would apologize: "Forgive me, Oh Saints!... I made an error, had dozed off." Scribes were not

immune to illness either: "I got a toothache: a tooth is a small bone, but a major malady." Only a few of them would admit that there were bright moments in their life as well: "Arsenije, the ecclesiarch, kept me going by providing good quality wine, may God forgive me!..." No one put the gist of the scribe's profession better than 14th century monk Stanislav, who noted: "The Grand Vojvod Oliver ordered that it be written, Stanislav wrote it."

Chilandar scribes never failed to refer to themselves as "sinful" or "humble" or "not worthy of mention." A number of them were not full monks, only "quasi monks" ("takha monach"). The monastic names of the scribes, i.e., of those who cared to divulge them, were Damian, Jov, Marko, Roman The Lame, Atanasije, Dionisije, Hegumen Dorotej, Pro-Hegumen Timotej. In the scriptorum they would have a few assistants, specialists of all kinds. These would help the scribes with darkening the letters, punctuation, coloring, and illustrations. Elaborate transcriptions and illustrations required team work. Ink preparation, parchment, special paper (bombicine) treatment, availability of good quality pens, book binding and scroll mounting - - all called for people with special skills.

Scribe Roman was a takha monach. In 1331, he transcribed *The Lectionary of the Gospel*. In 1360, lovely miniatures of the Evangelists were added to the script. A masterpiece indeed, the copy is among the outstanding works preserved in the monastery library. The 1331 transcript of the *Jerusalem Typikon* was Roman's work as well. The manuscript is now in Berlin. Jov, another takha-monach among the Chilandar scribes, was a tireless transcriber. Four of his 14th century transcriptions amount to over 1,300 pages of text. His copy of *The Chronicle of Gregory Amartola* brings out his exceptional fastidiousness: "... I wrote the way I found it in the original copy, nothing have I added or changed.. .." His copy of *The Lenten St. John Chrysostom* (c. 1385) ends with the pleading note: "... mention, Oh Man, the hand which wrote this." Jov's transcription of *The Sermons of Gregory The Theologian* ended up, of all the places, in Novosibirsk.

In 1356, "the year Tsar Urosh, the son of Dushan, died," scribe Dionisije finished his copy of *Tetraevangelion*. The manuscript is in the Chilandar library. Dionisije's shortened note indicates that he was a very devout person: "To the Trinity of the Father, and the Son, and the Holy Spirit — glory!" Damian's transcription of *John Chrysostom*, also in Chilandar's library, informed the reader that the original script was "in ruinous state." Damian found this particular manuscript so "powerful" that occasional gaps and missing pages did not bother him at all. "In case a better source-copy would emerge one day, this one might still be of use to brethren in monastery kellia," he reasoned.

In the 14th century there was a Chilandar scriptorum in Karyes as well. There, Pro-Hegumen Timotej transcribed *The Apostle* (c. 1360-70), which he called his "personal contribution to the holy ktytors (of the kellion)." Takha-monach Marko worked in Karyes where he copied *The Lives of Simeon and Sava* (c. 1360). The transcript had a disturbing odyssey in the 19th century when it was taken to Belgrade, subsequently misplaced, and finally found and safely deposited in the Belgrade National Library just before World War I. The German incendiary bombs that fell upon the same library in the Second World War (1941) burned down the building, including some 700 valuable medieval manuscripts. However, the fates seemed to have wanted Marko's transcription to be saved: a Belgrade professor had taken it home to study for only a few days before the attack!

There are 35 Karyes manuscripts in Chilandar today. Among them is Teodosije's *Octoichos* (13th century), and the famous *Tetraevangelion* presented to the Karyes kellion by King Milutin in 1316. In the 14th century, Karyes's workshop was as renowned as Chilandar's. The greatest medieval Serbian authors lived in Karyes and worked there at one time or another. Today, the visitor of St. Sava's kellion may walk over the overgrown ruins and foundations of the scriptorum. All Chilandar transcripts were done in the Serbian version of the Old Slavonic. The same is true of translations and adaptations. Thus, Chilandar scribes were setting the style, the language, and the grammar, later to be accepted in the widespread Serbian Diaspora of the Balkans. In the 17th and 18th centuries the Serbian version of the Old Slavonic was popular among Bulgarian clergy as well; Bulgarians found it easier to use than the Russian version.

Many of the books transcribed by Chilandarians found their way out of the Holy Mountain area. The demand was great, and the impact even greater. It seemed that Turkish occupation had not hindered the activities of the scribes. In the 17th century, Karyes scribe Averkije ("from Hercegovina") amazed his brethren by producing at least one *Panegirik* annually for five consecutive years (1622-26). His is also the high quality transcription of the *Book of the St. John Chrysostom*, (1632). The 18th century had its prolific scribe as well. His name was Teodosije (hieromonk), "Serb from Croatia." He must have made numerous transcriptions because seven of his manuscripts have survived and are still in Chilandar.

It would be improper to close this short review of the Chilandarian writers without mentioning the monk who became the fourth (and the sixth!) Serbian Patriarch. His name was Efrem, often referred to as the Patriarch-Poet. For some fifteen years he was a humble Chilandar monk, before moving out of the monastery, in search of absolute solitude. Although of Bulgarian extraction, he was highly respected in Serbia and considered a living Saint. He had a passion for writing Church poetry. He wrote many Church hymns, canons, akathistoi, kontakia, stichera and encomiums. The 14th century script in the Monastery Dechani titled *Vitae, Sermons and Wondermakings*, as well as the *Book of Canons* in Chilandar library, are both attributed to Efrem.

Finally, there is yet another self-effacing Mount Athos monk of whom little is known except that he wrote remarkably thoughtful verses. The author's monastic name was Siluan. History knows of two Siluans, living two centuries apart (14th and 16th), but is inclined to credit the former with the authorship of *Verses for St. Simeon* and *Verses for Sava*. Siluan had an amazing ability to condense meditative philosophy into few words, to play with words and to compose poetic phrases.

The seven lines he dedicated to Sava attest to it:

Fleeing glory, you found glory, Sava,

There whence glory appeared to your people.

The light of your people's faith, you scorned the light,

And thereby appeared as a beacon to all your people.

Excellence of mind [in your case] superceded loftiness of position,

Thereby achieving perfection beyond understanding.

These words of praise of Sava were braided by Siluan."

(The Serbian version of the seventh line reads:
Slova Slavi Save Splete Siluan.)

NOTES

1. Djordje Trifunovic, *Primeri iz stare srpske knjizevnosti*, (Belgrade 1967), p.51.

2. ibid., pp.29-46, excerpts.

3. Mateja Matejic, (with Dragan Milivojevic), An antology of Medieval Serbian Literature in English, (Columbus, Ohio 1978), p.64

4. ibid., p.74

5. Dimitrije Bogdanovic et al: *Hilandar*, (Belgrade 1978), p.52.

6. M. Basic, *Stare srpske biografije*, (Belgrade 1924), p.97.

7. Djordje Sp. Radojicic, *Razvojni luk stare srpske knjizevnosti*, (Belgrade 1924), p.117.

Chapter IX

TURKISH RULE

As the 14th century was about to fade away, the Holy Mountain monk scanning the horizon could hardly find a bright spot in sight. The likelihood of stopping the invading Turks seemed impossible, and the future of Christianity (at least in the immediate vicinity) was utterly bleak. Where was the monk to turn; whom was he to ask for support? The Byzantine Emperor and the Patriarch were entrapped in Constantinople, the city encircled and bypassed by the wily craft and stratagem of the brilliant warrior, Evrenos Bey. Two Byzantine Greeks found themselves outsmarted by a Turkish Greek. The Balkan Christian alliance was "blitzkrieged" before it could be organized. The Serbian resistance was in shambles, and Europe was frightened and growing increasingly apprehensive. With Evrenos's warpath cutting through the heartland of Serbia, the Serbian monk could only mourn over the fate of his nation.

Nobody expressed the sorrow better than the Chilandarian Isaija, who in his fading years had become the hegumen of the St. Panteleimonos Monastery. He was the same Hieromonk Isaija whom Emperor Dushan had met in Chilandar some 50 years ago... except that now, Isaija was the knowledgeable old man tediously working on the translation of the philosophical discourse of Dionisios Aeropagit, friend of Apostle Paul. Isaija was hoping to finish the work before departing this life. Grieving over the destiny of Serbia, author Isaija left a cryptic note behind. "This book I started in the good old times... finished it in the worst possible times." Then, sensing the short message to be inadequate, he decided to give his own account of the bad times.

Isaija's depiction of Turkish onslaught is brimming with dramatic imagery, yet, historians agree, the monk's rendition is incomparably more reliable and factual than numerous presentations written at that time with considerable liberty of interpretation. From the scholarly point of view,

that may be viable, but what appeals to the average reader, however, is
Isaija's style. He wrote:

> Surging Islamites swept over the land like flocks of birds. Some of the Chris-
> tians they (Islamites) put to the sword, others they took along as slaves... those
> who survived the onslaught later were let to starve to death; others, while still
> alive were turned over to the wolves to be devoured... Evil and the bereft per-
> meated our cities, and drenched our western regions, in ways that ears have
> never heard before, nor had eyes ever seen... the time had come when those
> living looked upon those dead as blessed with luck..."1

Sultan Murad II entered the city of Thessaloniki in 1430. The Mount
Athos monks lost no time in sending a delegation to the new master. The
Turk, in turn, promised to respect the religious autonomy of the community and to let the monks practice their religion. For their part, the
monks had to agree to pay a tribute, an imposition unheard of in the history of the Holy Mountain. What Sultan Murad II promised, Mehmed II
(The Conqueror) confirmed to the subsequent delegation that went to Constantinople in 1453, the year of the fall of the city.

These were unduly difficult times for the Chilandarians. Never were
their acceptance and popularity lower among the Athonites. The Mount
Athos monks were washing their hands of the Serbian brethren; the general
belief was that the ambitious Dushan was to be blamed for the weakening
of Byzantium. On the other hand, among the Turks the sentiment prevailed
that of all the nations conquered, the Serbs were to be the least trusted.
Although beaten into the ground, the Serbs were still perceived as potential leaders of resistance. Under the circumstances, what else were the
Chilandarians to do but lie low, endure, and wait for the storm to pass.

Serbian regional leaders, princes and despots (although many of them
Turkish vassals by that time) did not forget the Chilandarians nor did they
ignore their plight. Vuk Brankovic, "Master of Prishtina, Prizren and surrounding regions," took it upon himself to pay all the imposts pertaining
to Chilandar "metochia" and farmland in his area (1392). Vuk's concern
and sympathy for Chilandar were underscored by the fact that his own
brother Radonya was a member of Chilandar's community for three
decades (since 1365) as Monk Roman, and later as megaloschemos
Gerasimos.

In those wretched times, Vuk Brankovic and other Serbian grandees, in
a joint gesture of faith and loyalty, bought the ruins of the abandoned St.
Paul Monastery at Mount Athos and restored it. Gerasimos and another

Serbian monk, Antonios Pagasis (Antonije Bagash), helped St. Paul's regain the Athonite stature it has held ever since. After Vuk's death (1399), the story goes, Monk Gerasim went north to take the body of his brother, and bring it either to St. Paul's or Chilandar.

In the 15th century, the Serbian Despot Djuradj Brankovic (1427-1456), son of Vuk, reinstituted the traditional medieval funding of the Chilandar Monastery. The source of income was the famous Serbian silver mines of Novo Brdo (Montenovo). The mines were instructed to set aside one hundred liters of silver for Chilandar annually. This was in line with Dushan's budgeting of the Chilandar Monastery. He had ordered the Novo Brdo mines to provide 4,000 perpers per year. It is known that Prince Lazar supported Chilandar out of the same source until the Kosovo debacle (1389). In fact, the Novo Brdo source did not dry up untill after Sultan Selim II, in the wake of a strangling 40-day siege, finally took the fortified city in 1455.

In the 14th, as well as part of the 15th century, Serbian princes and despots aided numerous Holy Mountain monasteries. Thus, St. Athanasios's Lavra received 50 liters of silver from Djuradj Brankovic in 1427. Equally generous gifts were sent by Brankovic to the Esphigmenou Monastery in 1429. St. Panteleimonos's monks were known to have visited the widow of Prince Lazar (Militsa) in 1395. Her son, Despot Stephan, ordered 100 liters of silver to be appropriated annually to Chilandar , which made him the "second ktytor" of Chilandar in the family of Lazarevic (the first one being Prince Lazar, the builder of the narthex church of Chilandar's katholikon). In 1417, Despot Stephan Lazarevic ordered the Novo Brdo mines to send 60 liters of silver to the Vatopediou Monastery. Serbian noblemen Toma Preljubovic (Despot, 1367-84) and Vojvod Radich Postupovic (ktytor of the Kastamonitou Monastery) were among those who generously helped the monks of Mount Athos.

Rushing to the aid of Mount Athos were not only the leading Serbian men of the period, but distinguished women as well. History has yet to give full recognition to those brave Serbian ladies who had to step into the vacuum and shoulder the responsibilities of their decapitated, blinded, or perished husbands and male kin. Militsa, the widow of Prince Lazar, later known as nun Jevdokija (or Jefrosina), undoubtedly ranks as the dean of this benevolent corps. Holding a special place in the hearts of Chilandarians, however, is Mara Brankovic, the great-grand-daughter of Militsa. In the post-Kosovo period, Mara was given to Sultan Murad II (1421-1451). She was the stepmother of Murad's successor Sultan Mehmed II, the conqueror of Constantinople, who held Mara in great respect; as such she had considerable influence among the Turks. She had

used her title of Sultaness to force the City of Dubrovnik to resume pay-
ments of the so- called "Ston tribute" to Chilandar, the tribute instituted
by Dushan in 1333. It amounted to 500 ducats annually, and was the results
of Dushan's ceding of the fortified town of Ston and of the Peljeshats
peninsula to the Dubrovnik Republic.

The first two monks to go to Dubrovnik in the 15th century to collect
the tribute due were Arsenije of Chilandar and Cyril of St. Paul's, the latter being the second Mount Athos house of religion that "Mare Im-
peratritis" held in great favor.   When the two Athonites reached
Dubrovnik, a gold piece was broken into three parts.   One part was
deposited with the city treasurer and after that no tribute could be collected
unless the three parts of the coin matched. For centuries—until 1792—the
City Republic of Dubrovnik honored the charter signed by Sultaness Mara
in 1479. Today, one wonders how long the Dubrovnik City Fathers would
have played the coin game had they not been swept away by the surge of
Napoleon's tide.

Mara died in Serres (1487), not far from the Holy Mountain she loved
so dearly. The mountain that had turned her back when she personally
brought the Gifts of the Magi to the peninsula. The legend says that as
Mara landed, the tremor of the mountain warned her not to complete her
mission. Yet before departing this world, Mara did one more favor for
her monasteries by involving the Wallachian Vojvod Vlad IV into helping
the monasteries of the Holy Mountain. This, in fact, began the long tradition of Romanian patronage of the Mount Athos institutions.

Mara, the Serbian woman at the Turkish court, had her Serbian counter-
part among the Hungarian potentates. She was the wife of the blind Stefan
Brankovic (Despot in 1458), the last ruler of Serbia before the Turks over-
ran the country. Her name was Angelina (national tradition remembers
her exclusively as "Mother Angelina"). In today's context, the reference
is of enlightening interest since Angelina was of Albanian blood!

At the beginning of the 16th century, probably circa 1509, while
Chilandarians were still not out of their trauma,   Angelina wrote her
famous letter to the Russian Grand Duke Vasily III Ivanovich (1505-1533),
urging the Russian ruler to help the Slav monasteries of Mount Athos.
With the demise of Serbia, there is no one else to help them — Angelina
pleaded — the monasteries now "having no other prospective patron but
Your Highness." The Serbian Despotess reminded the Russian Grand Duke
that "Serbs have never separated the Roussikon Monastery from their own
Chilandar, and have on several occasions saved the Russian monastery
from Greek takeover." [2]   In her poignant letter, "the Despotess of the
vanishing Serbia transfers to the newly born Russia the burden of future

caring for the monastery founded by the ancestors of Vasily III" . At the same time she reminded the Tsar that this was an "all Slav" obligation, implying that now was Russia's turn not to "separate" Chilandar from Roussikon.

Vasily responded by sending a gift of Russian proportions as it included 200 ermine and 5000 squirrel pelts. Added to the shipment was the silver cup, suggested by the Despotess, so that the Holy Mount monks could toast the imperial benefactor befittingly. The Tsar, of course, was fully aware of the fact that quite a few of the Roussikon monks were of Serbian descent... One wonders if it ever occurred to the male-centered Chilandarians that, at the most crucial moment in their history, it took four gallant and courageous women to bail them out... That it took a female tetrad— i.e., Empress Jelena, Princess Militsa, Sultaness Mara, and Despotess Angelina— to extricate the Chilandarians from mortal danger.

Angelina was the one who opened a whole new horizon to the Chilandarians. There, over the vast tracts of Russian land— she pointed out— lies the yet untapped source of brotherly support. In 1550, Hegumen Pajsije, with three Chilandar elders in tow, reached the court of Vasily's son, Ivan the Terrible (1530-1584). Humble Chilandarians apparently did not seem dazed by the reputation of the tyrannical and gloomy Russian. Pajsije's courteous solicitation could not have been more heartfelt: "Today, all our monasteries of Slav language, which originally were established in [Orthodox] Greece, find themselves in foreign [Moslem] land; today, without our imperial ktytors, we are hungry and thirsty and naked." [4] Later, a third Chilandar delegation to Russia pleaded with the mighty Russian to convince the Turkish Sultan in allowing the monks to transfer King Milutin's remains from Sofia to Chilandar.

As a rule, Chilandarians were well received in Russia. Monastery delegates would spend up to seven years abroad before returning home. They kept moving from one place to another, primarily busying themselves with alms collecting, as well as delighting their hosts with Mount Athos stories. Tsar Ivan's dearest wife (of the seven he had), Anastasia, donated to Chilandar a beautiful altar curtain, the splendid needlework depicting Christ blessing the Virgin Mary and St. John the Baptist. Included among the miniature busts of Russian saints in the embroidered margin of the curtain are the images of St. Simeon (Nemanya) and St. Sava. Today the visitor is able to admire this magnificent piece of work in Chilandar's library building.

In the same library the visitor can see three gramatas (special charters) signed by Ivan the Terrible, one issued in 1551 and two dated 1571. The famous Tsar donated to Chilandar a "manor" in Moscow, which was to

serve both as a source of steady income and as a residence for Chilandarians when in town. In 1596, Ivan's son Feodor I, confirmed the status
of Chilandar's manor. In 1591, he signed a gramata authorizing Grigorije,
the Hegumen of Chilandar, to "supervise the restoration of Roussikon
Monastery".[5]

The Russian imperial support of Chilandar soon became a tradition;
numerous Russian charters saved in the monastery serve as testimony to
it.   One "Golden Seal" gramata was issued by Tsar Boris (Godunov)
Fedorovich in 1603, followed by the 1624 charter of Michail Fedorovich.
Aleksei Michailovich signed his charters in 1658 and 1660, and there are
those issued by Ivan and Peter (The Great) Alekseievich in 1684.

Altogether, six Russian tsars had come to the rescue of Chilandar in the
period when help was most needed.   However, Chilandar not being the
only Orthodox monastery in difficulty, the multitude of begging monks
knocking at the door soon became too great a burden, even for the treasury
of Russian proportions.   A system had to be devised by which all applicants for aid had first to "register" in a special book; aid was allotted
in fixed amounts and applicants stacked in terms of visitation time.   Thus,
Chilandarians were welcomed to come every seventh year and collect their
allotment of 100 rubles.   En route, as a bonus, they were permitted to collect alms.

There is no positive and firm data as to the number of resident monks
living in Chilandar in the 16th century.   Since this was the period of con-
solidation of Turkish rule over the Balkans, one would expect the number
to be small.   Most of the sources revolve around the total of 170 monks,
which would seem to point to a figure of 300 monks before the depletion
started.   What seems confusing is that at the time when debts were mounting, manpower subsiding, and difficulties of all kinds overshadowing, the
monastery went through a construction and restoration boom.   The 16th
and 17th centuries were periods of ambitious projects, the monastery itself a full-fledged hive of industry.   The main gate was remodeled, the
cistern for rain water and the aqueduct, as well as the laundry facility,
were finished; the refectory was restored, the hospital wing enlarged, and
the monastery's vast cellars, high walls and slate roofing, badly in need
of repair, were all fixed.   Extensive reconstruction work took place outside the monastery compound as well, notably at the Transfiguration Pyrgos in the hills (also known as "Spasova Voda").

Chilandar hegumens who feverishly pushed for the execution of these
works in the past are heroes of today's Chilandarians who strive to equal
or excel in deeds of similar kind.   The present-day Pro-Hegumen Nikanor,
in the monastery since 1927, considers the amelioration of the Kakovo

metochion, near the city of Yerissos, his greatest achievement since becoming head of the monastery.

 Pro-Hegumen Nikanor's hero is Genadije, the hegumen who built the
two storied guesthouse of Chilandar in 1558. Nikanor tells of another
guest-quarter building that was finished in 1598, the time of Hegumen
Teodosije. In 1634, Hegumen Philimon built the spacious entrance gate
of Chilandar and its iron-sheeted heavy doors. The parekklesion above
the entrance to St. Nichola's Chapel is credited to the perseverance of the
energetic and industrious Hegumen Victor (1661), who later had the chapel
frescoed (1667). Today, one can see the image of Victor on the wall of
the parekklesion, holding the model of a small church, in the tradition of
ktytors.

 Another hegumen, Simeon, is remembered among Chilandarians for his
role in saving the monastery in the 17th century from being either taken
over by the Greeks or auctioned by the Turks. The house was deeply in
debt and with no prospect of help in sight when Simeon turned to his
brother, a Venetian merchant, for assistance. The response was salutary;
the brother placed his wealth at the disposal of the monastery and he himself joined the brethren. He paid all the monastery debts and financed extensive restoration works at the Spasova Voda site, where he built the Holy
Trinity Chapel. Also, he insisted on replenishing the monastery library;
he provided the necessary funds and, in general, greatly enhanced the
morale of the dispirited and worried monks. In time, grateful Chilandarians elected the wise newcomer to the position of "spiritual father"
of the fraternity. The former Venetian, now Father Nikanor carried out
his delicate duties remarkably well, residing in his little chapel most of
the time. He died in Chilandar in 1685, and is remembered as "Father
Nikanor, the savior of the monastery."

 In retrospect, the Nikanor episode must have been more than a stroke
of luck. It helped the Chilandarians to take a new turn in their relations
with the outside world. All this took place at the time when Austria was
eager to create the "cordon sanitaire" along its southern border by en-
couraging a conglomeration of refugees and migrants to homestead in the
buffer-zone separating Europe from the Ottoman territory. Many of the
settlers were of Serbian origin. In time, their number grew to such proportions that they made a homogeneous enclave of their own. In this manner, the Serbian Diaspora had spread to the North, and outside the realm
of the Ottomans.

 Nikanor, the Venetian, must have had first hand knowledge of this new
enclave... of its economic potential, its social fabric, and its nationalistic
fervor. Less preoccupied with Moscow and Russian patricians than his

Athonite brethren, he must have concentrated on the new source which
was developing closer to home, more germane and comprised of kin folk.
In this sense, one can assume that Nikanor was the one who had gently
nudged the monks toward exploring the Serbian enclave in Austria.

The enclave and the monastery needed each other. With the Russian
support dwindling, the monastery had to find a new source. Serbian
homesteaders, at the other end of the spectrum, did not want to lose their
national legacy and needed support to fend off attempts of outright
proselytization. Thus, in addition to kinship, there were other objective
circumstances that helped the development of a strong alliance between
Chilandar and the Serbian Diaspora in Austria.

In the 18th century, until Maria Theresa in 1769 banned Turkish subjects from holding property in Austria, the Chilandar Monastery owned
"houses" in cities Novi Sad and Sremski Karlovci. Both properties
(metochia) were bought earlier by private citizens (Serbs, of course) and
donated to the Chilandar Monastery. The gifts must have reminded the
monks of their "manor" in Moscow. Yet, there was an important distinction, both in size and significance: the Moscow "manor" was a gesture
of solidarity, the two "houses" were a manifestation of patriotism.
Austrian citizens of Serbian descent were motivated by a compulsive national feeling of their own, to have a part of Chilandar in their hometown.
Those homes were always referred to as "Chilandar's House."

These citizens felt good about the fact that their Metropolitans — two
of them in particular, Vichentije Popovic (1713-25) and Pavle Nenadovic
(1741-68) — were stalwart supporters of the monastery. When Nenadovic
introduced the "Chilandar box" in local churches, citizens contributed
generously.

Partaking of the spiritual life of the Serbian enclave in Austria, Chilandarians sparked and fostered patriotic attitudes that later proved invaluable to "Mother Serbia," once it had regained its freedom. In the 19th
century, courageous freedom-loving peasants found a whole class of highly qualified and patriotic Serbs in Austria, willing to enter Serbia's public
service and help shape the fledgling province into a modern European
state.

The role of the Serbian Church, in general and of the Chilandar
Monastery in particular, in shaping the public opinion of the Serbs in
Austria is yet to be evaluated. There is no doubt, however, that the Serbs
on both sides of the Austro-Turkish border felt the same way. Although
the priests and ranking clergy belonged to two separate ecclesiastical juris-
dictions (Pech Patriarchate in Turkey and Sremski Karlovci in Austria),
they all perceived the role of Chilandar as an integrating factor.

Of the three Serbian spiritual centers, only Chilandar could afford to ignore parochial and jurisdictional limits. Chilandar provided coherence and coalescence the length and breadth of the all-Serbian movement, as the Diaspora spilled over territories ruled by three super-powers of the period. Chilandarians were the ones who were responsible for this achievement. After all, who else could have done it? Who else had the expertise in doing what Chilandarians did best: helping the nation to rise and stand on its own feet? St. Sava did it in the 13th century, and his disciples have never stopped treading the same path.

In 1720, Patriarch Mojsije (Rajovic) of Pech wrote to Vichentije (Popovic), the Metropolitan of Sremski Karlovci: "... the [Chilandar] monastery is ours and yours, it would be a great shame for all of us if others were to take it over." [6] In 1723, Patriarch Mojsije brought up the same subject in his letter to the National and Church Annual Convention of Serbs in the Monarchy ("the Sabor"): "Of all the past glory and the magnificence we once had... this [the Chilandar Monastery] is the only body of evidence we can show to other peoples and faiths as proof of our former eminence and fame, both imperial and patriarchal." [7]

Among the Serbs of Austria, the Chilandarians were not regarded as monks when on alms-collecting ventures. Rather they were perceived as holy men on a national mission. All doors were opened to them; they had free access to private homes, monasteries and churches, as well as palatial residences of Serbian leaders.

Those aged and venerated hegumens were viewed as walking symbols. When they officiated at Sunday morning service in the local churches, the parishioners felt history had visited their house of prayer. This feeling must have been shared by the Metropolitan of Sremski Karlovci as well. When the Chilandarians would call to pay their respects, it was he, the Metropolitan, who felt highly honored and who greeted the hegumen of St. Sava's monastery with utmost humility. In the reception hall of the Metropolitan's baroque palace, one was able to witness a spectacular scene of "Past" and "Present" in a brotherly embrace. It was a dramatic spectacle, but even more dramatic was what the meeting implied: the message of national awakening.

Quite a few of those greatly admired Chilandarians never saw their monastery again. They died abroad, their mission interrupted, but not discontinued. Soon, the monastery would send a replacement to pick up the trail. Elder Gerasim died in Sremski Karlovci, Pro-Hegumen Efrem in The Orahovitsa Monastery, Pro-Hegumen Arsenije in Vojlovitsa Monastery. Gerasim had an equivalent of 200 ducats among his personal effects when he passed away (1760). An accurate account, precise instructions as to what to do with the funds, and the Register of donors were passed on to the successor, Pro-Hegumen Pajsije, when he arrived. Pajsije was of Bulgarian descent, a highly respected and knowledgeable Chilandarian. Bulgarians know him as "Pajsije the Chilandarian" and consider Pajsije their first historian. He authored the first comprehensive account of Bulgaria's past (*The History of Slav Bulgaria*, 1765). Today, quite a few Bulgarian scientists and laymen find it difficult to separate the monastery from the monk, claiming both, i.e. author Pajsije and Chilandar, as being parts of Bulgarian legacy. They overlook the fact that Pajsije did most of his research in the archives of Chilandar Monastery, but wrote his book in Zographou Monastery much later.

Covering territories inhabited by Serbs all over the Balkan area, Chilandarians visited the various Serbian communities under Ottoman, Austrian, and Venetian rule. "Gathering in their churches, people would listen to the Chilandarians, hear the latest news, and learn about developments in other Serbian regions. All this would become the source of new encouragement and of the desire to endure...." [8] Chilandarians never came empty-handed; transcripts of old Serbian documents, St. Sava's vitae, charters adorned with royal signatures and, of course, icons and relics — were always part of their baggage. Hosts were always in a state of anticipation: what have the monks brought this time? Besides, Chilandarians made a point of making themselves useful during the visit by repairing old liturgical books, filling in or even writing missing chapters, acting as cataloguer or teaching the local young monk in the art of bookbinding. They advised the local hegumen on public relations, especially on coping with pressures of the predominant faith in the area, whether Moslem or Roman Catholic.

Serbian monasteries and churches in the areas of Dalmatia, Montenegro, Hercegovina and Bosnia treasure the memory of those visits. Even today, after a series of war plunders, many a psalter, icon, sacred utensil, vessel, and Athonite carved wooden cross may be seen as silent witnesses of those contacts. In northern Dalmatia, the name most often mentioned is the one of Mitrofan Bogdanovic, the Chilandarian who hailed from that area and often visited his native land. Another Chilandarian, Antonije, was made "Captain" of the Monastery Banja (St. George's); he and his Chilandarian friend, Monk Maxim, restored the monastery near Risan (Gulf of Kotor) in 1718. Chilandar's monk Athanasios brought to the Monastery Savina, near Hercegnovi, the famous upper-torso icon of St. Nicholas (1759), painted on Mount Athos. Dubrovnik's Serbian Orthodox Church display's a number of old icons, either brought by Chilandarians or acquired through visits to the Holy Mountain. In Hercegovina, the best known Chilandarian is undoubtedly Pro-Hegumen Victor, who had taken his monastic vows at the local Zhitomislichi Monastery and who had maintained close contacts with his native region. In 1667, Pro-Hegumen Victor paid for the fresco-work done in Chilandar's Chapel of St. Nicholas. Earlier, another Zhitomislichi monk, Milailo (died in 1645), was pro-hegumen of Chilandar Monastery. Bosnia's native son among the Chilandarians of fame in the 17th century was Pro-Hegumen Philimon.

The relationship between Chilandar and any given Serbian area was so strong that neither distance nor location were of significance. Local monks were encouraged to go on pilgrimages to Chilandar; there they would put to a test their dedication and devoutness by adhering to strict and austere standards required of a Chilandarian. Hardened and strengthened, they would return to their monastery enhanced and feeling like a graduate. Visits of this kind have continued to the present days.

As recently as October 1986, the baritone voice of Lazar of Ostrog Monastery rang beautifully in the vaults of Chilandar's main church, as he conducted nightly vigil services for a period of three weeks. This tall Montenegrin appeared at the gate of the monastery one late afternoon, laid away his pilgrim's staff, and rushed upstairs to greet the fatherlike figure of Pro-Hegumen Nikanor to whom he said reverently: "My soul is in need of recharging, Father, so I came...." One early morning Lazar, his inner strength renewed, was seen looking around for his walking stick. Minutes later the Black Mountain monk was hiking up the steep narrow trail into the Holy Mountain sunrise.

This Montenegrin had just visited the monastery which is some five centuries older than his own Ostrog (built in 1665). However, Lazar's idol, the Metropolitan of Hercegovina (Vasilije) who had built the Ostrog Monastery and is buried there, had demonstrated his love for Chilandar by restoring its pyrgos and the Chapel of St. George in 1671. Thus, he set an example for Lazar... to care always for Chilandar and perceive it as his own spiritual home, and to stand ready always to offer assistance, because the Chilandar Monastery has the unique distinction of belonging to all Serbs.

"The White Chilandar" as bards and minstrels referred to it throughout history, was always more than a church surrounded by a solid wall and pyrgoses. Tradition maintained that as long as "White Chilandar" stood so would the Serbian nation. When the greatest Serbian national hero King Marko died, who else but the "Pro-Hegumen Vaso of White Chilandar" found him "asleep under the tallest fir-tree of Mount Urvina." Where else would Vaso have taken the body of the dead hero but to the "Church of the Chilandar Monastery." And where else would the monk entomb King Marko but "in the middle of Chilandar's main church?"

Of hundreds of Serbian monasteries in existence, none has caught and held the fancy of the nation as Chilandar. What contributed to its captivating power was probably the humanness of the monastery, the fact that it embodied the whole nation. Throughout its history the monastery identified with its homeland, rejoiced, and/or grieved with the Serbian commonwealth. Although on foreign soil, the feeling of common bond and brotherly compassion persisted continuously; intertwined with mythology and legends, the mutual affection grew ever stronger.

Not a bit of this feeling has been altered. Today, a Bosnian visitor upon entering the Chapel of the Miracle of the Virgin's Veil ("pokrov"), heedless and remote as he may be, warms up instantly, as he is told that the Chapel was restored by the "sons of the Sarajevo Serbian Church" in 1740, hardly two decades after it was badly damaged in a blaze (1722). The abbots throne in the Katholikon, he learns, is the gift of Isaiah, the Metropolitan of Bosnia (1635). His chest filling with pride, the Bosnian senses he has come home, just as Montenegrin Lazar felt.

Those journeying from northern Dalmatia feel good when shown the large bell, a gift of the Zadar (Zara) general in 1785. Visitors hailing from Vojvodina examine with particular interest the "horugva" (church banner) sent by Bishop Jovan Jovanovic of Bachka (c. 1800). Belgradians are told that their Metropolitan Simeon (Ljubibratic) restored the chapel and the pyrgos of St. Sava in 1682. Many Macedonian names are found among the donors and those who made a bequest. Hosts of Serbs, from Pechuj in Hungary to Ohrid in the Southern Balkans remembered Chilandar when writing their last will. This commonwealth aspect of Chilandar is the element that makes it so stimulating and so widely acceptable. All Serbian visitors identify with the monastery; upon leaving they are in some sort of ecstasy, their hearts thrilling and their souls stirring.

Ask Pro-Hegumen Nikanor what produces the spark? "Faith"—he will say. "Faith in Christ?" you inquire. "No. Faith in Chilandar. The nation believes that 'as long as there is the Monastery Chilandar, Serbia will live'. . . . I guess people feel they have to come here, to convince themselves that Chilandar is still alive... and counting," winks the good-hearted hegumen.

Visitors' concerns, however, are not unfounded. It was only a century ago when, by an ironic twist of history, the monastery was in mortal danger of becoming de-Serbized. Chilandar, the provider of Serbian cohesiveness abroad, gradually was losing its Serbian character internally. In the 18th century the ratio of Serbian monks in the monastery was gradually the Balkans, the nation had to rush to the death bed of its exhausted and weakened partner. It took an entire century to save Chilandar from irreversibly losing its Serbian ethnicity and from forsaking the basic intent of Emperor Alexios' chrysobull of 1198, which specified that Chilandar "be given to monks of Serbian lineage in perpetuity." The struggle for admission of Serbian monks in the monastery is the subject of a separate chapter.

NOTES

1. Djordje Sp. Radojicic, *Razvojni luke stare srpske knjizevnosti, (Novi Sad 1962), p.163.*

2. Aleksandar Solovjev, *Histoire du monastere Russe au Mont Athos*, (Byzantion 8), p.16.

3. ibid.

4. Djoko Slijepcevic, *Hilandarsko pitanje u XIX i pocetkom XX veka*, (Cologne 1929), p.453.

5. Dimitrije Bogdanovic et al: *Hilandar*, (Belgrade 1978), p.134.

6. ibid. (English language edition), p.176.

7. Djoko Slijepcevic, *Istorija srpske pravoslavne crkve*, Vol. I, (Düsseldorf 1978), p.495.

8. Dusan Kasic, *Manastir Hilandar i njegov znacaj u srpskoj istoriji*, (Millenium volume on Mount Athos) (Belgrade 1961), p.28.

Chapter X

THE AILING MONASTERY

Ask a Chilandarian today to review the history of his monastery: never will he tire of referring to the times of glory; he may not mind analyzing periods of defeat, but he definitely will turn uneasy and agitated if he is asked to discuss the 19th century. This was the century when the Chilandar Monastery was a multinational community. Ethnically, it was a mixture of Bulgarians, Serbs, occasional Russians or some other Slavs, even a few Greeks. At that particular time, such a mixture of nationalities could bring only frustration, incoherence and chaos. No Chilandarian wants to be reminded of the times when in his religious house the resident monks spoke different tongues.

In the Balkans, the 19th century was one of rampant nationalism. The much acclaimed solidarity of the Slavs, heretofore an advantage, had turned into a liability. Serbs and Bulgars in the monastery were on a collision course, mainly because their homelands (with their turbulent histories) were poles apart. Eastern Orthodoxy and the Holy Mountain "synthesis," Slavic kinship— all this could not hold back the feisty nationalism. After all, were not the Greek monks in just as much a nationalistic dither as the Slavs were? Was it not the Holy Mountain that gave shelter to the leaders of the Greek national uprising in 1821?

For quite a long time Chilandarian monks tried to resist outside influences and pressures. However, the monastery could not afford the luxury of total insulation. The monks needed help, a lot of it. The stern reality was that the Turks had ceased to regard the Holy Mountain as the place of prayer, but rather as the nest of revolutionaries.

In the monastery, pondering Chilandarians were caught between Serbian claims and Bulgarian ambitions, between two opposing national strategies and assertive foreign policies. Two capitals, Belgrade and Sofia, had begun their tug-of-war over Macedonia. The embroilment over Chilandar be-

105

came inevitable because the national affiliation of resident monks in the monastery had become a major issue, as it was constantly shifting to the advantage of non-Serbians. At that particular time, Chilandar was populated mainly by Bulgarians and Macedonians, the Serbs being a minority. Serbia, however, continued to claim the monastery on grounds of a well-known medieval connection; Bulgaria, on the other hand, insisted upon the actual status.

It is fair to say, that in the begining, the nationality issue was of no concern, because the monks felt foremost as Chilandarians. For quite a while, the consensus prevailed that Chilandarians should stay above politics. However, as pressures mounted, the consensus eroded; some monks left Chilandar, others took sides and became involved in the squabble, still others tried to play both sides. No matter who did what, it was "un-Chilandarian."

At that time most of the visitors reported that the Serbian character of Chilandar Monastery was doomed. They should have known better. Obviously, those wayfarers knew little about the true nature of the Mount Athos inhabitants. Monks, in general, are not prone to giving up, particularly those of the Athonite type, and especially if they happened to be disciples of St. Sava. It is true that throughout the 19th century the Serbian monks in Chilandar were a minority; actually, a steadily dwindling minority. Yet they endured. They believed that St. Sava, their Patron Saint would not let them down. He guided them in times of Turkish supremacy at its zenith; they felt St. Sava would not abandon his children in the period when Turkish supremacy was fading away.

There was another factor, undoubtedly more tangible; in the 19th century, Serbia—the homeland—was free again. After two national uprisings, the liberated nation was seeking recognition, more or less as Sava once did. There was no way that at such a crucial moment the resurgent nation could afford to lose its foundation, its own past,the precious legacy deposited in the monastery. In all of old Serbia, liberated or yet to be freed, no other monastery was endowed with such a deeply seated mystique, such a wealth of cultural and historical mythology, as the "White Chilandar on the Holy Mountain." Therefore, as long as there remained a single Serbian monk in Chilandar, he could rest assured that the renascent Serbia would not forsake either him or the sacred home of Nemanya and Sava.

The same degree of confidence and faith reigns in Chilandar today. Indeed, it explains the optimism and the morale of the monks. Father Arsenije, today's inhabitant of Chilandar, explains it in terms of interaction: Each Chilandarian is but a second in the history of the monastery. He amounts to a blink in the entirety of Chilandar's existence. Yet, short as it may be, he [the Chilandarian] provides the notion of continuity, of the linkage... of the necessary connection sought by pilgrims. He reassures the visitor [from Serbia] of the vigor of his nation... Thus, as confidence in his nation's past and in his own is rekindled, the pilgrim departs fearless...."

It works the other way too, as Pro-Hegumen Nikanor says, "there is nothing that fills my heart with greater joy than the sounds of the Serbian language echoing through the spaces of these vast hallways and stairways..."

The binding force that exists between the monastery and the homeland was expressed in a rather moving way when, at the time of the Serbian First Uprising against the Turks (1804-1813), the Chilandar's Pro-Hegumen Danilo sent the carved wooden cross to the insurgents. A decade later, upon the collapse of the liberation attempt, the Orthodox peasants made sure the cross was returned to the monastery (1814), for fear it might fall into the hands of the "infidels."

Later in the 19th century (1826), the Chilandarian Onufrije Popovic, Bulgarian by birth, called on Milosh Obrenovic, the leader of the fledging Serbian province. The educated Bulgarian had come to plead with the illiterate leader of the Serbian peasantry. Onufrije was a freedom fighter just as Milosh was; he had to leave the Holy Mountain because of his involvement in the Greek uprising. He told Milosh of the difficult times that had befallen the Holy Mountain monasteries; he expected Milosh to emulate the magnanimity of Serbian medieval noblemen and to come to the rescue of Chilandar.

The leader of the deeply Christian Serbian peasants could not refuse the honor. Yet, it took a while before Milosh could afford to act as a donor. In 1835, he had sent 100,000 groshen to the Holy Mountain, along with his own precise instruction as to how the money was to be distributed. He assigned 5,000 groshen to each of the five leading monasteries,(including Chilandar); 4,000 groshen to each of the 15 remaining monasteries; the largest skete was given 4,000 groshen while nine others got 3,000 each. Milosh had not forgotten the hermits living in their austere caves and huts, he set aside 1,500 groshen to each one of them. Perhaps Milosh could not match the magnitude of an Emperor's gifts, but the gesture was undoubtedly on par.

When there was no Obrenovic around, the tab was picked up by either a Karadjordjevic or the Serbian National Assembly or both. In 1847, Prince Aleksandar Karadjordjevic induced the National Council toappropriate 500 ducats annually for Chilandar. Available records show that

Serbia had continuously provided aid to Chilandar. Throughout the 19th century, Serbia budgeted 300-600 ducats annually, or an equivalent amount, for aid to Chilandar.

For two decades, Milosh's friend Onufrije Popovic corresponded with the Serbian Government on the subject of support for Chilandar. Half of that time he operated out of Constantinople as some kind of special assistant for Chilandar affairs. He was in direct contact with the Ecumenical Patriarch on this matter, in constant touch with Russians and western diplomats, as well as with Belgrade, of course. Part of his correspondence, as later published by another Chilandarian, offers a fascinating insight into the modus operandi in the Ottoman capital at that particular period.

Most of his time in the Moslem city, Onufrije spent in the ante-chamber of the Ecumenical Patriarch, waiting to be received for an audience. The cunning Greek must have been intrigued by this lucid Bulgarian acting as counsel to the Serbian Government. There was one thing that both men had in common, however: they lived dangerously and walked on thin ice among the Moslems.

Both were under the veil of lingering suspicion, because the Turks were still angry about the role of the Holy Mountain in the Greek Rebellion. In 1821, the Patriarch's predecessor carelessly had betrayed his feelings; he was unceremoniously hanged by the neck at the main gate of his residence. Painted black, the gate was never to be opened again, or at least as long as the Turks were in town. His soul must have been hovering around that conference room at the time the two Athonites discussed the destiny of Chilandar.

Onufrije Popovic returned to Chilandar in 1856, after being officially advised that his services would not be necessary any longer. Serbia had formed a special committee to deal with the matter. In Constantinople the Chilandarian bid good-by to the Serbian envoy, on whose payroll he was barely surviving in the capital, and went back to the anonymity of a monk, but he was never to be forgotten by the Serbian nation. In 1854, artist Urosh Knezevic made a masterfully executed oil-painting of Archimandrite Onufrije, the valiant national spokesman. Onufrije thus became the first Chilandarian known to sit for a portrait.

Another Serbian artist involved with the Chilandarians at about the same period was Dimitrije Avramovic, muralist and heraldry expert. In 1847, he was dispatched to the Holy Mountain by the Princely Office of Public Education. He stayed on the Holy Mountain for two months, three weeks of which he spent in Chilandar. His assignment was to register "Serbian historical documents" in the libraries and archives of the Holy Mountain monasteries. Avramovic took his assignment very seriously. An artist with personal interest in medieval costumes, he possessed an exceptional sense for detail, and never tired of searching. After two months, he had only one complaint: the reluctance of the monks to bring to the light of the day "those valuable documents!" Nevertheless, what he was able to reveal to the nation, in terms of old books, medieval manuscripts, valuable relics and icons, gave a heartwarming boost to the morale of those who labored to save Chilandar. Avramovic noted: "... in my humble opinion, the Holy Mountain must have many more Serbian literary documents than I was able to see." He wrote this in his report to the interested nation, later published in book form. Today, Serbian historians of all kinds unanimously commend the artist for giving them the first meticulously prepared point of reference.

In the 19th century, the Chilandar Monastery seemingly had not had a single period of respite from serious financial worries. Obviously, whatever support was offered by Belgrade was not adequate. This had compelled Chilandarians to take up alms collecting. Since such activity required the securing of an official permit, Chilandarians felt, and rightly so, that Belgrade would be the last one to turn them down. Apparently, at one point (1853), the pleas for help were so great in number that Belgrade Metropolitan Petar became apprehensive about the limit of Serbia's benevolence. He pleaded with the Department of Education of the Principality of Serbia not to deny the Chilandarians permission to collect alms, even if their requests were more frequent than reasonable. The Metropolitan reminded the Department that of "all former Serbian regions, once ruled by the glorious Nemanjices, only our Principality has its own political life and independence," which left no one else but Serbia proper with the burden of supporting Chilandar.

The Metropolitan was overstating his case, because as we already know, the Serbian Diaspora outside of Serbia had come to the aid of Chilandar rather readily. But no department in the Principality would question the authenticity of the pronouncement by the Metropolitan. The permit was issued instantly.

In 1856, two Chilandarian monks reported to the Metropolitan of Belgrade:

> As for the concern shown in view of our (Chilandar's) distress, and the compassion expressed for the Holy Mountain by the people of Serbia, we are lacking the ability to describe them adequately; we can only say that the Serbian people entertains great admiration and affection for its holy places, loving them zealously, with pure heart and flaming soul, thus keeping alive the tradition set by their Serbian ancestors."[1]

As a result the monks had returned to their monastery with 200 ducats in cash.

Unfortunately, regardless of how crucial the collection of alms was for the survival of the monastery, the money seldom remained with the monks. As the "sick man of the Bosporus" got ever sicker, so were taxes getting ever higher. On the other hand, as Chilandar was becoming weaker internally (due to the discord and partisanship), the monastery's possessions were falling prey to aggressive local landowners, Turkish bosses, and even brotherly monasteries. The protracted and ruinous lawsuits that followed—some of them lasting for decades—used up most of the alms collected and threatened to bring the monastery to foreclosure. A combination of heavy taxes, legal expenses and unavoidable customary bribes, reaching as far as Constantinople, prevented the monks from dedicating their time to prayers. They found themselves frantically engaged in the daily affairs of the materialistic world.

Under such circumstances, Chilandar's Bulgarian hegumens appeared to be an asset. They had a reputation for being first-class managers. Their nationality had helped them to approach Bulgarian masses and to broaden the support base of the monastery. During their period, intermittently a time span of well over 100 years, they won the good will of numerous Bulgarians. In Chilandar, considerable restoration work had been carried out by hegumens of Bulgarian descent, notably Archimandrite "Daniel of Gabrovo" (second half of the 18th century), who set the example for others to emulate him.

In the tradition of hegumens in Russia, Bulgarian hegumens tried to leave a personal mark by either improving the general status of the monastery or adding a structure during their tenure. The names of Bulgarian hegumens are neither kept secret nor forgotten in Chilandar. Today, one can find Bulgarian hegumens depicted on the walls of Chilandar chapels, as well as the names of Bulgarian donors. . . names of humble, but very generous people; names of small town folks and villagers who went on pilgrimages and who called themselves "haji" - - people like Vlcho of Bansko, Cvijetko of Vidin, Petko of Morevenik. Cvijetko provided the necessary funds for the gilding of the iconostasis in King Milutin's Church of Chilandar (1774). A year later, Vlcho restored the badly damaged parekklesion of St. Stefan. He dedicated it to the Bulgarian national patron Saint, John of Ryla. There was nothing unusual about having the "Chapel of St. John of Ryla" in Chilandar; the Ryla Monastery, near Sofia, still has the "Room of St. Sava."

For centuries, Serbian and Bulgarian saints could inhabit each other's
monasteries without being the cause of agonizing restlessness among the
monks, or exacerbating relations amoung friends of the monastery. By
the middle of the 19th century, however,it became painfully evident that
on the Holy Mountain the nationality issue had outranked sainthood. Gone
were the days (10th century) when the Greek confessor, Athanasios, and
Georgian noblemen could build their monasteries (Lavra and Iveron)
without jealousy and rancor in their hearts. Or when Nemanya could
easily win the support of Greek Athonites to build Chilandar (12th century).

The ongoing internal struggle for control over Chilandar was mainly the
result of the wider political Serbo-Bulgarian rivalry. But, this conflict was
not the sole bone of contention on Mount Athos. Involved to a greater
degree were other nationalities, through adversities of their own on a larger
scale. The ever increasing presence of Russian monks on the Holy Mountain was causing considerable anguish among the Greeks. It was not long
before the Greeks viewed the Mount Athos situation in terms of " natives"
versus "foreigners," their alarm boosted by concern among western al-
lies.

Typical of the Russian mode of intrusion were the cases of two poverty-
stricken small Greek communities, the Vatopediouian skete of St. Andrew's
and the Pantocrator's dependency of the Prophet Elijah. In 1841, two
Russian monks settled at what was known as the Kellion of St. Andrew's.
In 1845, Tsar Nicholas I sent his son (Grand Duke Constantine) to lay the
foundation stone of the church that was to replace the kellion. In 1900,
the Russian Admiral-in-Chief of the Black Sea Fleet — with the blessing
of the Ecumenical Patriarch — led the procession of international dignitaries attending the consecration ceremony at the magnificent onion-
domed church, the one that still dominates the outskirts of Karyes. As for
the skete of the Prophet Elijah which in 1800 had only two Russian hermits, it was soon housing 300 Russian monks, praying in the Russian language in their most beautiful church.

A similar transformation was taking place in the St. Panteleimonos
Monastery. After being in Greek hands for more than a century (1735-
1840), the monastery was bought back by the Russians. Hegumen
Gerasimos was in great need of cash to pay the accumulated monastery
debts, and the Russians had made a tempting offer. In time, they paid a
total of 800,000 piastres, enlarged their numerical presence in the
monastery, and obtained the right to celebrate the liturgical services in both
Russian and Greek (this tradition is still maintained in the monastery). In
the end, the aged Gerasimos was replaced by the controversial Russian

hegumen (Makari Sushkin). It took five years to have this election approved by the Ecumenical Patriarch (Joachim II) and the Holy Synod in Constantinople, but the trend proved irreversible. Greatly intimidated, the Greeks alleged that bribe money and graft were heavily used in the transaction. Some thought that the charge came from "experts in greasing the palm" and therefore out of place.

St. Panteleimonos Monastery continued to grow in size and in number of resident monks, but not in influence over Mount Athos affairs. The monastery had reached the monstrous proportions, accommodating over 1,000 monks, but it had never become the "leading monastery." This, of course, meant that St. Panteleimonos's hegumen could not discharge the duties of the Holy Mountain Protos.

Thus, in the second half of the 19th century, the Serbian monk in Chilandar was faced with three simultaneous developments, and he frankly could not see how any one of the three could help him. He was faced with a) the Bulgarization of his own monastery; b) the Russification of the Holy Mountain; and c) the growing Greek resentment of all "foreigners," including the Serbs.

There was no question that the most harrowing of the three situations was the Bulgarization of Chilandar. With despair and a heavy heart, the Serbian monk recalled that Emperor Alexios III had originally approved of building the Chilandar Monastery for the use of men of Serbian nationality.

As for Russian upmanship in the Aegean area, this was of lesser concern to a Chilandarian, mainly because of traditionally good relations with the Muscovite Orthodoxy. With regard to the Greek antagonism, history had shown that attitudes of that kind were subject to fluctuation. As a rule, whenever forced to choose between the Serbs or the Bulgars, the Greeks would opt for the Serbs, seemingly the lesser of two evils.

As it happened, at this particular point in time, the Russian Foreign Office was plainly more interested in promoting Bulgaria than Serbia. Undoubtedly, the geographic location of Bulgaria has played a decisive role in this policy. The Chilandarian knew that "Matushka Russia," for reasons of political expediency, might at times pay more attention to one of their "Slav children" but would never totally forsake either of them. After all, Russia had fought four wars against the infidel Turks in the 19th century alone — and just as many in the 18th century; hardly could such a nation ignore the Serbian cause. Yet, it was Russia that extracted the Bulgarian autonomous Exharcate in 1870 from the reluctant Ecumenical Patriarch; and it was Russia that dictated to the Sultan the Peace Treaty of San Stefano in 1878 — both moves considered so blatantly anti-Serbian by the ruling

Prince Milan Obrenovic that he hurried into the fold of Austria. Upheavals of this kind, however, could not shatter and destroy traditional ties. Serbia's ecclesia had never severed or discontinued its own liaison with the Office of the Moscow Patriarch.

By the time the Serbo-Bulgarian controversy over Chilandar had peaked, Russian scholars — many of them ecclesiastics — were fully aware of the crux of the contention over Chilandar. Ever since the Russian "hiker" ("pjeshehodets"), Vasily Grigorovich Barsky, had visited the Holy Mountain (in 1725 and in 1744) and had written about the "Trojeruchitsa," King Milutin's church, the art work in the refectory of Chilandar, as well as about Serbian medieval charters in Lavra, Vatopediou, Iveron, Esphigmenou — no temporary policy consideration could have altered the basic Russian affection for the Serbian monastery. Discoveries made by Barsky were only the beginning of Russian scholarly interest in the "Serbian Lavra." Scores of Russian historians visited Chilandar since and have written extensively about the "Serbian Monastery." In 1847, Victor Ivanovich - Grigorovich of the Kazan University reported extensively on his findings in Chilandar and Karyes. Porfirii Uspensky, probably the most famous Slavic scholar of his time, visited Chilandar on three occasions within a period of 14 years (1845-1859). More often than not, rightly or not, Uspensky decided that the Holy Mountain documents had a better chance of survival in St. Petersburg and Moscow, which gave him a dubious reputation in the West. The Russian Archimandrite Leonid (L.A. Kavelin) also visited Chilandar and St. Paul's. In Chilandar, the Archimandrite found the situation to be "very deplorable." Some of his findings were also published in Serbian language in Belgrade (1877).

The person who did the most to focus the attention of the outside world on developments in Chilandar undoubtedly was the Belgrade Metropolitan Mihailo. A forceful personality, he exerted a strong influence upon Serbian public opinion. He had excellent connections in Moscow as well. British theologian and author, Athelstan Riley, met Mihailo (at that time "ex — Metropolitan") in Chilandar in 1884. Riley described Mihailo as a "clean-looking, well-bred old man, with a gentle face and silky beard... (he) did not look at all like a man who had recently mixed himself up with political intrigues to the extent of defying his sovereign... King Milan (Obrenovic)."

According to Riley, Mihailo and the Holy Synod of Serbia, fearing the consequences of Milan's

subjecting himself and his infant Kingdom to Austrian instead of Russian influence... to the Latin instead of Orthodox ally, violently opposed the King,
who finally deposed the whole bench with a stroke of his pen and obtained
fresh prelates from the Orthodox Church in the Austrian dominions... How far
he [Mihailo] had acted from purely religious in opposition to political motives,
and whether or not he was a mere puppet in the hands of intriguing Russia, I
am not sufficiently well acquainted with the quarrel to say, but will merely
repeat that his manner and appearance impressed us favorably.[2]

It was during Mihailo's term that the Chilandarians were trying to re-
establish their old ties with Russia; the office of the Belgrade Metropolitan
was used as the most effective conduit. Chilandarian requests revolved
around the permission to collect alms in Russian territories. But there
were some more ambitious plans as well, like the request to be allowed
to open a "chasovnia" (Chilandar's manor) in St. Petersburg. In 1863,
Chilandarian Sofronije died in Russia while on an alms collecting mission;
a year earlier, Chilandarian Isaija had perished in a shipwreck. Being of
service to the Chilandarians, Metropolitan Mihailo felt free to dispense of
some useful advice too. In 1863, Mihailo suggested to the Elders to revert
to coenobia in the monastery in order to tighten the internal discipline and
rekindle the old spirit.

In 1866, Archimandrite Gerasim wrote to the Metropolitan that the
coenobitic system was abandoned, that Chilandar was hit by at least three
collateral lawsuits, and that debts were mounting at an alarming rate. -
"... because of all those most difficult circumstances, which have a
paralyzing effect on Chilandar, we have sunk into deep despair," the Archimandrite bewailed.[3]

The worst was yet to come. With the rise of Bulgarian nationalism in
the 70's, and the corresponding assertiveness of the Bulgarian monks in
Chilandar, the Belgrade Metropolitan had to plead with the hegumen of
St. Panteleimonos (Makarije) to make an attempt to bring the [Bulgarian]
brethren of Chilandar to their senses, and hopefully "save our Chilandar
Monastery." There was even talk of renting one Chilandar skete to the St.
Panteleimonos Monastery. Nothing came of it, but in 1876 Hegumen
Makarije confirmed to Mihailo that "the Serbian element in this family
[of Chilandar] was very small indeed, no more that two or three per-
sons..."[4]

Throughout this difficult period, Chilandar had its standing delegate in
Belgrade (Monk Visarion), constantly pleading with Serbian sources for
financial aid. Exact figures vary, but there was no uncertainty about the
seriousness of the situation, and the urgent need for support. There is no

doubt that in the period of the 1870's, Serbia had come the closest to losing Chilandar.

One might wonder, why would the Bulgarians (and their temporary Russian supporters on the Holy Mountain) be concerned about the ownership of Chilandar when they both had their own monasteries on Mount Athos? The answer is simple. Neither one of their two monasteries — Zographou and St. Panteleimonos — had the rank of "leading monastery." They needed Chilandar for only one reason: the opportunity to send their hegumen to Karyes. Chilandar loomed as the possibility and as the opening to reach for that otherwise unattainable office of the Protos.

Russian attempts to wield influence on Mount Athos are not the subject of this book; those efforts have been covered amply in related literature, mainly by western authors. It is easy to see how the Russians would have profited had their clients (Bulgarians) secured regular access to the office of the Protos. To many a Russian, as citizen of the mightiest Eastern Orthodox country, gaining influence at Mount Athos, the Center of Orthodoxy, looked quite cogent. The irony of it was that, were it not for the Bulgarian angle, Serbia probably would have supported the Russian drive fully. However, as already indicated, the Bulgarian ambitions to gain control over Chilandar made such support inopportune. Belgrade had to undertake resolute steps to finalize the ongoing dispute. The best Serbian minds became involved in the search for workable solutions to the problem. Several Serbian envoys in Constantinople (historian Stojan Novakovic, statesman Jevrem Grujic, and diplomat and publicist Dr. Vladan Djordjevic) were frantically engaged in this "Save Chilandar" campaign, which took a few decades to accomplish.

In the 1880's, after Serbia had gained full independence and was internationally recognized by the Berlin Congress, it became clear that sovereign Serbia could not tolerate half measures any longer. In 1882, Archimandrite Nikifor Ducic, at that time the Head of the National Library in Belgrade, arrived in Chilandar. He was a prominent figure in Serbia, member of the Parliament, member of the Serbian Academy of Learning, and, at one time, the Chief Custodian of the National Museum. In Chilandar he was on a semi-official fact-finding mission.

For a man of his background and stature this must have been a very exciting trip. In a report submitted to the Academy, and later to the nation, he recalled the surge of emotion that "filled my soul." Being a historian and an ecclesiastic, Ducic's "flesh tingled," as he realized that he was walking on the same path that Saint Sava and Nemanya walked in medieval days and that he was about to enter the most famous of all Serbian libraries, containing numerous charters and chrysobulls signed in scarlet, and that he would be able to examine illustrated (decorated) Gospels and see the marvelous medieval needlework (an altar curtain) embroidered with golden threads by the Serbian Princess, nun-Euphemia. The visitor's heart was filled with excitement which was difficult to describe: "No penmanship could give account of it" , wrote Ducic.

In his report submitted to the Committee for Governmental and Historical Sciences of the Serbian Academy of Learning, Ducic's opening statement read:

> To arrive at Mount Athos, sojourn in this earthly paradise, see for yourself the great Serbian Lavra, the famous Chilandar, bow piously at the grave of Saint Simeon Nemanya, pace the soil once walked upon by most illustrious Serbs... and then not tell a single word about Chilandar, for a Serb, it would be sinful.[5]

Ducic's report was an account of a special envoy on a national mission. That particular October, the Archimandrite was not on autumnal vacation taken to satisfy his own cultural or spiritual needs. In a letter dated May 12, 1884, to the historian Ilarion Ruvarac (another cleric-historian), Ducic admitted with disarming candor: "I was not in Chilandar because of old books and scholarly research, but for entirely different reasons." [6] He went there as a personal envoy of Metropolitan Teodosije (the one who had replaced the exiled Mihailo) to evaluate the internal situation, and to make sure that the managing of monastery affairs was in line with "the spirit of St. Sava's Typikon."

As for the nationality of resident monks, Ducic confirmed what other visitors had stated, notably the Serbian educator Dositej Obradovic, as early as 1765 ("I found only few Serbs in the monastery, interminably quibbling with Bulgarians, unable to agree whose monastery it was.") In 1882, Ducic established that "at present, 80 monks reside in the monastery, most of them of Bulgarian nationality; hardly one tenth of the monks are of Serbian descent...."[7]

One correction should be kept in mind though; at that time many Macedonians were willingly or unwillingly lumped together with one of two nationalities, Serbian or Bulgarian. In 1890, a visitor wrote to Metropolitan Mihailo: "There are 50 monks in the monastery—one Rumanian, three Czechs, and the rest of the brethren are Macedonians who take special pride in declaring themselves as being Bulgarians."[8]

Metropolitan Mihailo listened to complaints of this sort patiently, maybe even saw some relevancy in them. Undoubtedly, they made him even more determined to work for a clear-cut resolution of the Chilandar problem. By that time, official Belgrade had clearly passed from tolerance to the offensive. Serbian consuls in Thessaloniki were instructed to keep in close touch with the monastery, to support the Belgrade proteges, and to assert the Serbian affiliation of Chilandar at all times. Serbian bishops were dispatched to visit the monastery; delegations of Chilandarians were invited to Serbia. Royal audiences were accorded to visiting Chilandarians, as well as ceremonial receptions, awarding of medals, promises of new patronages 97 all this became part of the carefully choreographed protocol in the last two decades of the 19th century. At least on one occasion, the Chilandarian elders had decided, unknowingly in Belgrade, to return to the monastery via Sofia. The maneuver did not sit well with either of the capitals, which felt manipulated by the monks. They, on the other hand, cited the two metochia the monastery had in Bulgaria as a pretext for visiting Sofia.

Balancing acts of that sort could not be tolerated much longer. Belgrade refused to accept "Slavic" and "economic" explanations as valid excuses, and made it clear to the Chilandarian Elders that, in the future, corresponding with Serbian authorities in the Bulgarian language would not be tolerated either. Typical of the short shrift was the tone (of the rebuff) attributed to the Serbian Consul (Ivan Pavlovic) in Thessaloniki, who in 1896 reminded the monks that since they had "of their own will accepted the hospitality of the Serbian monastery, the House of Simeon and Sava," common decency demanded that they make an attempt to master the Serbian language.

The definite pro-Belgrade sway of the monastery was assured after Serbian King Aleksandar Obrenovic had visited Chilandar in 1896. There, he celebrated the Eastern holidays with the monks. The King was on his way to Athens for a royal visit with George, the King of Hellenes. In Chilandar, Aleksandar Obrenovic pledged to consolidate all monastery debts, mortgages and liens (10.000 ducats), thus freeing the monks of financial worries. This, of course, gave Belgrade considerable clout and control over monastery affairs, and had strengthened the hand of the Serbian monks, those already there and those who were about to come.

At the turn of the century, two Serbian bishops were at the forefront of Belgrade's drive. Dimitrije Pavlovic of Shabats and Melentije Vujic of Negotin were working hard, in and out of the monastery, preparing the ground for the inevitable transition. First, they established good relations with the Bulgarian element in the monastery. Dimitrije was particularly well regarded among the resident monks. His good standing in Belgrade made him a natural choice for the job of an effective liaison. More often than not, he could be seen commuting between Chilandar and the capital of Serbia. But he also went on trips to Constantinople, Sofia, and Karyes. He found the Protos in Karyes friendly, the Patriarch in Constantinople well disposed, the Turkish "kaimakam" agreeable, and even the Bulgarian capital resigned to renounce Chilandar. With so much good will manifested on all sides, the mission could hardly fail, provided the whole affair was handled with tact and moderation.

Indeed, the process of repossession was remarkably peaceful and smooth... a rather civil and quiet affair, with a sense of a deja vu event. After all, how many times have the Mount Athos monasteries changed hands? Causes were different: attrition, bankruptcy, human destruction of the monastery, or natural disaster. Chilandar itself was built on the ruins of a previous monastery, and a host of religious houses on the mountain had been restored and temporarily inhabited by Serbian monks. Some monasteries were saved from extinction, thanks to last-minute help from the least expected quarters — Islamic patrons! Thus, when the time had come for the Chilandar Monastery to reassert its Serbian character, the Mount Athos monks took it as something destined.

The monks' attitude made an impact on Belgrade. Bishop Dimitrije Pavlovic wrote to the Chilandar Elders—still the majority of them Bulgarians—in 1900: "... leading circles in Serbia are very impressed and grateful to you for the calm and noble manner in which you have brought the Serbian Foundation back on its historical track, the one chartered by the holy ktytors."[9]

Actually, the true Bulgarian concern for Chilandar deserves a greater recognition than this sketchy review might suggest. In 1897, when some Bulgarian hotheads hinted that the visit of the Bulgarian King (Frederic) to Chilandar would now be in order—to counteract the effect of Obrenovic's gesture—the Prime Minister of Bulgaria rejected the idea as outlandish. To him, as well as to many members of Sofia officialdom, it was quite apparent that a Coburg would not fit in the Home of Nemanjices.

On the other hand, the Serbs readily admit that Chilandar was home for numerous Bulgarian patriots and national protagonists. Some of Bulgaria's most famous sons lived there, like Pajsije the Chilandarian (in the 18th Century) and the Bulgarian patriot Neofit Rozveli (in the 19th Century). The latter even died in the monastery (1848), confined there by the Turks for his sharp style of writing that inspired the revolutionary fervor of broad Bulgarian masses. It so happens that, to a Bulgarian, Chilandar is not just another walled-in Balkan monastery, but the sacred home of some Bulgarian national heroes.

Today, almost a century after they had returned Chilandar to the Serbs, the Bulgarians still care for the monastery. Serbo-Bulgarian relations on the Holy Mountain are very good and cordial. The two monasteries, Zographou and Chilandar, are neighbors, as their two homelands are. Today, young Zographou monks can be seen dismounting their mules at the gate of Chilandar and rushing up the steep wooden stairway to greet Pro-Hegumen Nikanor. The white-bearded man delights in such visits. Occasionally, the youthful guests would prod the host to speak about "Bulgarian" times in Chilandar. With a characteristic twinkle in his clear blue eyes, the pro-hegumen would address the subject directly. His most favored story would take the attentive listener back to the year 1883, the year when the Serbian Metropolitan Mihailo visited Chilandar. "In this very room"—Nikanor would relate—"flanked by all those Bulgarian elders who resided in Chilandar at that time, the Metropolitan of Serbia received the Hegumen of Zographou, who had come to pay his respects to the visiting Serbian dignitary." Then, pausing for a second, so that his young audience would have time to fully envision the scene, Nikanor would add: "You know, my children, strange are the ways of the Holy Mountain... Nathaniel, the Hegumen of Zographou, he was of Serbian blood!"

NOTES

1. Djoko Slijepcevic, *Hilandarsko pitanje u XIX i pocetkom XX veka*, (Koln 1979), p.36.
2. Athelstan Riley, *Athos or the Mountain of Monks*, (London 1887), p.183-4.
3. Dj. Slijepcevic, *Pitanje*, p.54.
4. ibid., p.56.
5. Nicifor Ducic, *Starine Hilandarske*, Glasnik SUD 56, (Belgrade 1884).
6. Dj. Slijepcevic, *Pitanje*, p.93.
7. Ducic, *Starine*, p.25.
8. Dj. Slijepcevic, *Pitanje*, p.116.
9. ibid., p.177.

Chapter XI

MODERN ERA

Serbia or the largest part of it was free from Turkish rule for one entire century, while Chilandar and the Holy Mountain still had to endure the Turkish Governor in Karyes. The monks had to deal with Turkish judiciary, Turkish police and army, as well as Turkish tax collectors. In one respect, the Turks seemed to be rather tolerant; fanatical Moslems were reluctant to interfere directly with affairs of faith. November 2, 1912, finally brought an end to all this. On that day, troops of King Constantine of Greece liberated Thessaloniki. The Mount Athos monasteries and the Mountain entered a new era in history.

It was a dream that had finally come true; however, at least as far as the Greeks were concerned, a dream that brought new worries. The Holy Mountain had turned away from the Ottomans, but Russians were there instead—many more than any Greek would care for. As a matter of fact, by 1912, "the Russians," had gained possession of one monastery, four sketae, 34 kellia and 187 hermitages of the Holy Mountain, with the numerical majority of the monastic republic."[1] According to prevailing estimates, the Russian presence was directed at as many as 4,000 monks. Probably included in this figure were other Slavs, such as Serbs and Bulgars. For the Greeks, the latter were always counted in, because they led to a wider concept of the "danger of Slavicization of the Holy Mountain."

In Western quarters, there was talk of a "Russian Gibraltar" in the Mediterranean. At the same time there was little that could be done either through diplomatic channels or military avenues. Article 62 of the Berlin Treaty, which seemed such a good idea before, now had backfired. In 1912, the mind of any diplomat in the West must have cringed when reading the grandiloquent text of 1878: "The monks of Mount Athos, whatever their country of origin, shall be maintained in their former possessions and advantages, and shall enjoy, without any exception, complete equality of rights and privileges."

In their monasteries on Mount Athos, however, the monks did not worry about diplomatic semantics. They were in a festive mood, euphoric about the arrival of freedom after a five-centuries-long waiting period. Indeed, who could blame them for the hosannas and alleluias exulted in their salutes. The atmosphere of a happy holiday gripped the Holy Mountain, monastery bells could be heard ringing loud, banners (of " Hellas") could be seen unfurled all over the peninsula.

Authors describing the scene often quote the reaction of the Turkish Governor ("kaimakam") in Karyes, as originally reported by a French interlocutor:

> "Look at these thousands of monks"- the disgruntled Turk allegedly said. "Of what, in reality, can they complain? Have we touched their rules? Have we violated their property? Have we forbidden their pilgrimages? Have we altered even a title of their secular constitution? What race, I ask you, what conqueror could have treated these people with greater humanity, greater moderation, greater religious tolerance? Under our law they have remained no less free, indeed freer, than under the Byzantine Emperors... And they have not had to endure under our domination a hundredth part of the vexations that you have imposed on your monks in France... Allez, Monsieur! They will regret us. Greeks, Russians, Serbs, Roumanians, Bulgars, all those monks hate each other like poison. They are bound together only by their common loathing of Islam. When we are no longer there, they will tear each other to pieces...".[2]

Indeed, very soon, freedom brought some disappointments. In 1922, Greece made an abortive attempt to reconquer Ionia ("the cradle of the Hellenic civilization") from Turkey. Later, in order to take care of 250,000 Greek refugees who arrived in Thracia and Greek Macedonia, the Greek Government expropriated huge tracts of land possessions owned by the Mount Athos monasteries. Chilandar lost some 3,000 hectares. It seemed as if the Turkish kaimakam of Karyes, in his fit of anger, was not much off key in his forewarning.

In the meantime, diplomats worked on the future status of the Holy Mountain. The map of the world had drastically changed after World War I; three emperors and one sultan had left the world scene. In the end, after three peace parleys (London 1913, Sevres 1920, Lausanne 1923), the Holy Mountain was internationally recognized as a" Greek Protectorate"(1924), and embodied as such into the Greek Constitution (1926).

This made every Chilandarian on Athos a Greek citizen (subject), but ex-
empt from taxation, custom duties, and military service. He was guaranteed autonomy in running monastery affairs. Ecclesiastically, he remained
under the jurisdiction of the Ecumenical Patriarch in Constantinople, always a Greek, and still in the Muslim city (Istanbul).

All this did not markedly affect Chilandar's relationship with Belgrade.
With the opening of the 20th century, the last vestiges of Bulgarian influence in the monastery were fading away rapidly, and Serbia was warm-
ing up for its imminent role as a Balkan Piedmont.

By a strange coincidence, at the very time that nationalistic euphoria
peaked at home, the most prominent monk in the Serbian Chilandar was
a monk of Czech nationality. He was Slavibor Breuer of Kutne Hozy, the
self-taught librarian, whom history remembers as "Sava Hilandarac"
("Sava, the Chilandarian"). Being a foreigner, hailing from Central
Europe, he was able to evaluate the situation in the monastery with the
calmness and the logic of a stranger. The European in him provided the
acumen and the foresight badly needed at that time among Chilandarians;
he was not the product of Byzantine thinking. In contrast to attitudes
shown by other Athonites, Sava was sensitive to comments and reactions
as expressed by foreign visitors, many of whom had a genuine scientific
interest in the cultural fund of Chilandar. Their comments, if and when
solicited, were usually negative in one respect: they all complained of the
lack of a systematic record of books and documents in the monastery.

Sava undertook to solve this problem. In 1897, he was able to put
together the first modern-type catalogue of Chilandar's "literary wealth."
He worked in "the room above the refectory porch." His first catalogue
listed 600 old manuscripts (130 of them in the Greek language), as well
as some other items. Later (1906-08), he moved his "office" to the vaulted
room (with ironclad door and windows) above the monastery's main gate.
There he kept the medieval charters and other selected manuscripts safely locked. There he prepared his second catalogue with additional entries
and his classification method improved. Each manuscript carried a stamp
of his own design, with the code number of the entry clearly marked.
Sava's codification, in spite of some shortcomings, helped scholars in many
ways; most of all, it allowed for an easy access to documents of specific
interest.

"Sava the Chilandarian" was an author in his own rights as well. At
the time when Slavic studies were flourishing in Central Europe, Sava
published in Prague (1895) an essay on Chilandar manuscripts—*Rukopisy
a Starotisky Chilandarske*—which was highly acclaimed. At that time,
most of the data on Mount Athos documents were reaching Europe via

Russia. Sava's report was exceptionally valued as coming from the source. A year earlier (1894), Sava's enchanting description of his beloved monastery was published in Belgrade. The booklet was a monumental success, leaving many a Serbian reader spellbound. Today, just as enticed, Chilandarian monks constantly refer to the booklet. The little volume is their most favored reading selection, the gem of their library. Sava's more detailed book on the subject of the Holy Mountain— *Kniga o Svate Hore*— was published in Prague in 1911. Also, Sava was the author of the German language essay on Onufrije Popovic and his famous correspondence with Serbia.

For some reason, Europe, was nicer to Sava the Chilandarian, than was Belgrade. Serbian academicians never cared much for this self-taught monk, with no degree in library sciences. They found Sava an inadequate scholar, they questioned his findings, they constantly insisted on his re-checking his own data. The good-humored Czech took all this in stride, endlessly corresponding with "savvy" members of the Serbian Academy. In 1911, the academicians finally mellowed, and agreed to publish Sava's monograph on Chilandar. The decision was late in coming; the same year Sava had passed away in Chilandar.

Sava's death would have created a great problem for Chilandarians were it not for the fact that he himself had trained Father Mihailo to continue in his footsteps. Dedicated and diligent, Father Mihailo— Milan Komatovic before taking the monastic vow— turned out to be a very efficacious librarian. Rummaging through the monastery's lofty corners, deserted kellia, remote chapels that had fallen into disuse, as well as many a dark and unexplored nook and hiding place in the monastery's cellar, Mihailo left no stone unturned. His effort paid dividends. This humble and unassuming member of the fraternity had added some 160 personally rescued titles to the monastery catalogue. Quite a few of the documents were dangerously close to being totally deteriorated, some of them survived only in fragments. The methodical researcher did not hesitate to comment and expand on data relevant to the entry; today, these personal annotations make for fascinating reading per se.

In 1926, Mihailo moved the Chilandar Library to a safer place— the building that houses the Chapel of the Holy Archangels. In the meantime, Belgrade had provided the necessary funds for the purchase and installation of proper book cases, shelves, and one heavy iron safe.

Today, as teams of cataloguers of the Serbian National Library come to the monastery to do the codification and indexing of Chilandar's cultural repository, they are enormously grateful to Sava and Mihailo, the two classifiers, not by profession, but by vocation. Mihailo left an indelible mark in the history of Chilandar. His nomenclature of monastery manuscripts still serves as a point of departure to scholars who conduct contemporary research projects in Chilandar.

Postwar scholars—in fact ever since the 1930s of this century—historians and bibliographers, specialists of all kinds (in the Slavonic alphabet, medieval music, iconography, Turkish documents, etc.) in their trips to the monastery, head straight for the office of the librarian. The names of Father Arsenije (until 1970), and Father Chrysostom (since 1971) are never to be forgotten by those eager visitors.

Today, Chilandarians are the first to admit that scholars in general have done incomparably more for Chilandar than any other category of people, including ecclesia or literati. Nowadays, as one visits the Byzantology Institute of the Serbian Academy of Sciences and Arts (SANU) in Belgrade, one hears Chrysostom's name mentioned repeatedly. Byzantologists of all over the world, including the United States of America, keep in close touch with the Chilandar Monastery librarian. One may note an interesting result of this comradeship with the monk: female academicians, who had never been allowed to visit the Holy Mountain, demonstrate the same degree of congenial fellowship with the faraway Chilandarian.

Chilandar's new Library Building (1963-70), indeed the gem of years-long copious and expansive restoration work carried out in the monastery under the supervision of Professor Slobodan Nenadovic, has brought modern age and its technology into the monastery's ancient surroundings. Designed to fit its environment perfectly, with all features of the interior carefully controlled (lighting, humidity, temperature, etc.) — the building has became the envy of the Holy Mountain. It harbors the most precious treasures of Chilandar: icons, manuscripts, and objects of art. The building is now ready to house the entire collection of over 30,000 printed books, which at this moment are being catalogued by teams of librarians from Belgrade, as well as to accommodate the needs of the ever greater number of visiting scholars.

Not to be underestimated is the interest of United States academe in Chilandar. In fact, the interest is of such scope that it deserves much more than a passing remark. In 1969, Professor Mateja Matejic of the Slavic Department of The Ohio State University in Columbus, Ohio, visited Chilandar and discussed with monastery elders the idea of an undertaking which subsequently became known as the Chilandar Research Project. The ambitious project, first of its kind in the history of the Holy Mountain, represented a conscientious effort on the part of an American academic institution to preserve Chilandar's cultural treasures. This out-

side effort was fully and unreservedly supported by the guardians of the
depository.

History is replete with instances of the destruction of cultural heritages,
observes Professor Matejic in the concluding remarks of his publication
The Holy Mountain and Hilandar Monastery.[5] He notes that in 1240, Tartars burned down the city of Kiev; in 1812, Napoleon set Moscow ablaze;
in 1941, the German incendiary bombs turned into ashes 700 old Serbian
manuscripts in the Belgrade National Library; in 1956, the entire library
of St. Andrew's on the Holy Mountain disappeared in flames. Fires have
enveloped the walls of Xiropotamou, Zograpghou, Chilandar, and other
monasteries in the recent history of Mount Athos.

Professor Matejic was allowed by the Chilandarians to photograph-
"every single manuscript and each document in Chilandar... any book he
considered valuable, the icons, frescoes, crosses, embroideries, architectural objects, and anything representing a historical record or cultural
monument."[4] The financial support for Matejic's extensive work was
provided by The Ohio State University, the American Council of Learned
Societies, the National Endowment for the Humanities, and the Serb National Federation, Pittsburg, Pa. It took four lengthy sojourns to the Holy
Mountain, and a span of some six years of work at home to complete the
project.

In the Spring of 1970, Professor Walter Craig of the Department of
Photography and Professor Matejic spent six weeks in Chilandar. In the
course of these six weeks they photographed 139 complete manuscripts,
hundreds of imperial and ecclesiastical edicts and charters, and a large
number of icons, frescoes and other objects of religious art. In this first
phase of the project, some 36,300 frames with approximately 72,600 pages
of manuscripts and edicts were recorded, of which about one thousand
pages were copied on color film.

There is another American, this one associated with Harvard University,
who is held in high esteem and remembered in boundless gratitude by the
Chilandarians. The late John Seymour Thacher, Director of Dumbarton
Oaks Research Library and Collection in Washington, D.C., was a frequent visitor to the Chilandar Monastery. Among the monks, John Thacher
is known as "Brother John"— brat Jovan— so close did he get to the hearts
of Serbian monks.

They recall that seldom would he arrive alone, usually in the company
of an American iconographer or art historian, or some kind of expert
with particular skills of great use to the monastery. Pro-Hegumen
Nikanor had a soft spot for this American Episcopalian from the very
moment they first met. On the first encounter, John arrived with a res-

torer of icons. Both of them had spent a number of days in and out of Chilandar, visiting other monasteries as well, when one day John suggested to Nikanor that he should indeed let his friend work on some soot-covered icons. Nikanor agreed on the spot, but pointed out that the monastery would not be able to compensate the artist fully and deservedly for the services he rendered. "You should have seen the expression on the faces of those two Americans" — says Nikanor. "They both jumped to their feet, and exclaimed incredulously: 'Compensate?... Do you realize that other monasteries charge for the privilege of being allowed to touch their icons?'..." This was news to Nikanor, but in a silent expression of Athonite solidarity, he left the question unanswered.

Today, Nikanor likes to tell this story in order to illustrate the caring attitudes of John Thacher and to explain, at least in part, how he came to feel so much at home in Chilandar.

There is another instance when John Thacher graciously showed his goodwill toward the Chilandar Monastery. John was the one who took it upon himself to pay for the expenses incurred by the monks' decision to silver-plate Nemanya's sarcophagus in the monastery katholikon. Not only had "brother John" financed the purchase of material needed—80 pounds of silver and 2 pounds of gold—but, in addition, he had funded the actual schooling abroad of the artist, the talented young Serbian dentist, recommended by the monks to do the job.

It was a sad day in Chilandar when word reached the monastery that John Thacher had passed away. In their church they held a memorial service; the monastery's missionary publication *Hilandar* (No. 7) carried the following obituary note:

JOHN'S PLEDGE

John's first visit took place in 1952. As he stepped off the Chilandar warf, at high noon, he fell in love with the monastery the moment he saw it. He told us he was the Director of the Byzantine Studies Institute (Dumbarton Oaks) in Washington, D.C. Also, he had spent considerable time in Constantinople, Jerusalem, and on Mount Sinai in the pursuit of preservation of Greek cultural documents and icons. Because of his expressed interest, but in particular because of his outgoing personality, we showed him far more than is customary. Having seen the disrepair and deterioration of building and our cultural treasures, he pledged that upon his retirement he would dedicate the rest of his life to Chilandar. At that time, we regarded his pledge as a bit unusual. Afterwards he came yearly. Among his suggestions, one was for us to build a new

library on the very same spot where the old building stood till it was consumed
by fire in 1722. When, in 1963, we indeed did take his advice and began construction, he sent us a substantial sum of money.

One day, Brother John brought along a team of conservationists to restore our
old icons of incalculable artistic and historic value. To date, the monastery has
150 such icons, restored and preserved, which now may be venerated and ap-
preciated by many pilgrims.

Every year John spent two months in Chilandar, intending to become an in-
tegral part of the brotherhood of monks. We all remember the day when John
came up with the idea that the monastery should have a new sarcophagus made,
worthy of our Father Simeon Nemanya, to replace the old deteriorated one.
He offered to bear all expenses.

Even when absent from the monastery, John always thought of Chilandar. In
the Washington National Cathedral, he had one stained glass window installed,
which represents the Eastern Orthodox icon of St. John the Forrunner.

As years went by, John grew older together with us. How often, he wished to
overstay the Karyes - authorized visits!

John Tatcher was selected as one of the six distinguished speakers at the dedication of the "Hilandar Room," instituted as part of the Library of the Ohio State
University in Columbus.

Brother John maintained steady correspondence with us throughout the years.
He was always interested to know about all the monks, and what was happen-
ing to them.

In February, the news of John's death reached us. Soon after we were informed
by his solicitor that the Chilandar Monastery was included in his last will and
testament. Brother John had left a five-digit sum (in U.S. dollars) to the
monastery, twice the amount he had left to his own Episcopalian Church in
Washington, D.C.

This, in short, would be the "Chilandar biography" of our Brother John, which
we submit in his honor and memory. We pray daily that the Lord may grant
our departed *ktytor* to dwell in the Heavenly Kingdom of His Love."

There is a moving handwritten entry datelined May 18, 1980, in
Chilandar's *Guestbook VIII*, which reads:

"For nearly thirty years I have been coming to Hilandar. It has now become
my second home and more important, my spiritual home. If only all the world
could follow the example of this Holy Place."
(Signed) John Thacher

The list of American Chilandarians would be incomplete without mention of Vadim Cherny, the last descendent of the 17th century Serbian
Patriarch Arsenije III Charnojevic. In 1690, the Patriarch led a massive

exodus of some 35,000 Serbian families across the border to Austria, in the wake of failing Austrian military campaigns on Turkish territories. Much later, some of the Charnojevices moved to the Ukraine, wherefrom they branched to America. The Americanized Charnojevic, Vadim, was a builder of bridges and oil rigs, and apparently a man of means, who, as he grew older, felt an urge to retire to monastic life. Visiting the Holy Mountain, he set his heart on Chilandar.

One day in April of 1981, a chartered helicopter circled over Chilandar, landed in the small field adjacent to the monastery wall, and made Vadim's wish come true. One would think he had come to live his last years away from the hassle of construction sites. It turned out that he had come to die in Chilandar... He did not have years, months, or even weeks left to live; it was a matter of a few days. In his lungs, the malignant tumor was choking him.

Two strong monks, Vasilije and Pajsije, carried Vadim into the monastery on a stretcher. The next day in hardly an audible voice, he made his monastic vows. Speaking in Russian, he asked the pro-hegumen of the Serbian monastery for his fatherly blessing, for the prayer and for the absolution of sins. What an ending to a bizarre story: three hundred years after leaving Serbia, and nine generations later, the last Charnojevic, returned home.

Today, in the tiny yard of the 14th century burial church dedicated to the Annunciation, the pilgrim may hear Father Vasilije mention that Vadim was "the third biggest donor to the monastery, after the kings in the Obrenovic and Peter I Karadjordjevic families." In his testament, Charnojevic had stipulated that part of his bequest be used to fund the Collection of Printed Books of the Chilandar Library.

NOTES

1. F.W. Hasluck, *Athos and its Monasteries*, (London 1924) p.60.
2. John Julius Norwich et al: *Athos*, (New York 1966), p.84.
3. Matejic's book was published by OSU, Columbus, Ohio, 1983.
4. Matejic, ibid.,p.80.

Chapter XII

IN LIEU OF CONCLUSION

There are 15 monks in Chilandar today. Most of them hail from the heartland of Serbia ("Shumadija"). Dedicated disciples of Saint Sava, prideful of the place Chilandar has had in the history of the Serbian people, they view themselves as guardians of the Serbian national heritage. The way Father Mitrofan puts it: "We provide custodianship free of charge." At the same time, he says. "Hilandarians have an irresistible sacred desire of their own, i.e. to get as close as possible to Lord Jesus Christ; as vividly and as closely as Peter, James, and John experienced it with Him on Mount Tabor, in the miraculous event of Transfiguration."[1]

The cognizance of this particular spiritual aim is not always fathomable to the visitor of Chilandar. On his mind, there is another question: how long can 15 monks last out in their custodianship? The pilgrim is horrified to learn that at the time Pro-Hegumen Nikanor joined the monastery in 1927 there were 71 monks in Chilandar. During World War II there were 40 monks. This diminishing trend shows a steady line and leaves an indelible imprint in the mind of the outsider. Perturbed, he may even raise the issue with Nikanor, only to find out that a Chilandarian never fails to put up a courageous front. "Someone, somehow will bail us out; somebody always did come to the rescue of the monastery," says Nikanor, "it happened repeatedly in the history of Chilandar. Trust in God...."

Since 1973, 500 novices have come to the Holy Mountain. Many of them young, under 30 years of age, mostly of Greek nationality. Their mean level of education was unusually high, never before seen on the Holy Mountain. Of those 500 newcomers, only five came to Chilandar. A frightfully small number, especially when one realizes that twice that many Chilandarians have passed away in the same period of time. Today, the population of the Holy Mountain monasteries is estimated at 1,500 monks, many of them in sketes, kellions, and dependencies. Fifteen Chilandarians make just one percent of that monachal total.

Sketes and kellions are quite popular among the newcomers. It offers greater flexibility in application of monastic vows. Also, these young monks are not "fugitives," they do not come in order to "escape" the modern world and its amenities, but rather to make use of the opportunity of seclusion. Father Panteleimon of Chilandar, the young novice from West Germany, says: "I came to pray for the world as it is today. Don't you think there is a lot to pray for?"

Generally speaking, Slav monasteries are the ones which feel the rejuvenation crisis more drastically than the Greek houses. Nikanor semi-dejectedly admits: "For some reason, young Serbs come and leave; Greeks stay."

There are those who unequivocally blame Greek immigration policies for the lack of young monks in Slav monasteries, as well as Greek attitudes toward countries with atheistic regimes. They blame discriminatory quota regulations, double standards in visa treatments, and—most all—an alleged "Greek desire to achieve ethnic purity on the peninsula."

Slavic phobia (if existing) is not the subject of this book. However, Chilandarians become annoyed indeed when they are reminded by Athens that, in future official references, their monastery should be called "The Holy Mountain Monastery," not "The Serbian Monastery on the Holy Mountain." Details of that sort, apparently, grate the nerves on both sides. Chilandarians insist that ever since Emperor Alexios III authorized the founding of their monastery, it has been known as "The Serbian Imperial Lavra of Chilandar."

As of recently, since Greece joined the European Economic Community, visitors and monks from member-countries enter Greece (and the Holy Mountain) without drawn out visa hassles experienced by citizens of Eastern Europe and Russia. Certainly, Nikanor must find it frustrating, and indeed ironic, that an Orthodox monk from West Germany had an easier access to Chilandar than the Orthodox monk from Nemanya's Studenitsa.

In principle, Greek insistence that monks residing on Mount Athos be considered Greek citizens is of no concern to Chilandarians. However, Serbian monks on Mount Athos, as well as Slav monks in general, find it unacceptable that they be required to relate to their native people according to concepts of another nation, i.e. the Greek nation, or that they be expected to sever all connections with their homelands. In such a case their existence on Mount Athos, the "Home of All Orthodoxy," would lose its real meaning.

As for the future, imminent or long range, Chilandarians do worry, but are not in a state of panic, as some outsiders suggest. Nikanor's main concern remains the problem of insufficient replenishment of his monachal flock. He is hoping, however, that the two Governments (Greek and Yugoslav) will be able to work out some arrangement that would not impair future injection of new blood. Every now and then, one may hear about a sneaky Greek ambition to take over Chilandar, to gain its earthly wealth and its land possessions. Chilandarians refute this kind of talk; they prefer to believe in fair play and in what is known as "Anthonite solidarity." After all, Chilandar is one of five "leading monasteries," it provides the Holy Community with the Protos every fifth year, it wields considerable influence among the monks, and Chilandarians, as individuals, command great respect.

Chilandar's Pro-Hegmen Nikanor held the position of Protos in 1963, Mojsije in 1968, Mitrofan in 1978, Chrysostom in 1983; the Protos for 1988/89 again is a Chilandarian Father Pajsije. All this makes the Chilandar Monastery fully involved in Mount Athos affairs. As far as loyalty to Mount Athos is concerned, the Chilandarians have an impeccable record. There have been 35 Chilandarians discharging the duty of the Protos since the present system of governing was introduced at the end of the 18th century. Some of the Chilandarians served two, even three, successive terms. Others held the post at crucial times indeed: Pro-Hegumen Sinesije in 1821, the year of the Greek National Uprising; Archimandrite Makarije in 1878, the year of two relevant Peace Treaties (San Stefano and Berlin); Pro-Hegumen Kliment in 1914, the year of the First World War; Hieromonk Dositej and Pro-Hegumen Arsenije during World War II.

The general upkeep and economics of the monastery are on very solid ground. Its glorious past has made Chilandar one of the wealthiest, if not the wealthiest monastery of the Holy Mountain. It owns 8,000 hectares of choice Mount Athos real estate, with 30 kilometers of coast-line. Most of this land is forested, including the sector richly endowed with the red-chestnut, much in demand as first-class home construction timber. The monastery owns a number of "methokia" outside of the Holy Mountain as well. The Greek Government is still repaying the monastery for land expropriated in the 1920's, and the Yugoslav Government sends in a yearly equivalent of 1,000.000 drahmas to the monastery. "We do not need money, we need young blood," says Nikanor.[2]

As previously stated, the future is much on the mind of every Chilandarian. Father Vasilije, representing the thinking of the younger generation in the monastery, in the fashion of true Athonites, likes to dispell the anguish with the parable:"In the 14th century, a Catalan force of

1,000 men surrounded the monastery. They split in two units, 500-strong each. As they got ready to attack, a heavy fog set on the valley. In the ensuing battle, Catalans mistook each other for enemies; only three of them survived the bloodshed. Soon the weather cleared up, the three witnesses of the miraculous event fell on their knees, and begged the monks to let them join the fraternity. They are still with us," beams Father Vasilije," depicted on the wall, above the door of our old refectory as Manuel, Savel, and Avil...."

The story expresses the deeply seated belief that no matter how bad the situation may turn, at some point in time, somehow "Our All-Holy Three-handed Virgin Mary will save her monastery from evil and danger," solemnly states Father Pajsije.... in this monastery, every liturgy starts with asking for Her blessings; every project seeks Her approval, every trip abroad Her godsend; every business arrangement is made in front of Her icon (no signatures required): every internal dispute is brought to Her attention and resolved in Her presence...." And, says Mitrofan to a bewildered visitor,"You may not always understand us, you may even feel sorry for us, as we often feel sorry for you... But please bear in mind that for you to understand us, you should have lived *our* life, as we lived *your* life before donning the black rasson."

There is no doubt that an exposure to the Chilandarian leaves a deep mark upon the visitor. He walks away a different person. If anything, he walks away humbled. When the pilgrim first enters the monastery ossuary, and his eyes gaze upon the rows of hollow eye-sockets, the skulls of former generations of monks seem silently to beckon: "...linger a while so that we may reveal to you our marvelous mysteries, and show you the path toward your own secrets, which, unless you come to recognize and live accordingly, you shall never die, because you are already *dead*."

These skulls have a way of making the Serbian visitor drop whatever measure of cynicism and/or derision he had brought with him. Impulsively, he realizes he is being judged: is he worthy of the silent dwellers in this crypt?. He is confronted by the peers of the living pro-hegumen. At that moment, they are tabling the question Nikanor would refrain from asking, lest he might embarrass his guest.

This is the bare bone of how the pilgrim feels, and what he experiences upon his visit to the monastery. What counts here is not what he brings with him, but rather what he carries away as he takes leave from the Chilandarians.

There is many a skeptic who would challenge the mysterious powers of spiritual healing through merely visiting the monastery. On the other hand, there is a moving testimony that soundly refutes the disbeliver, expressed

by the Serbian poet Matija Beckovic in 1987.   Face to face with
Trojeruchitsa, whom he calls "instantenous helper" and "Mother with three
palms of the hand," the poet eloqunetly presents his case:

"... Here only, Oh Heavenly Tsarina,
Infinite prayers are spoken in my tongue,
No lies are told, no meat is eaten,
And fasting lasts eight centuries.
Should ever my homeland and native tongue be erased
All but for the spot on which I stand now,
I know: we have not quit mankind as yet,
For as long as there is You, I too live on."

NOTES

1. Moma Dinic, interview with Father Mitrofan *"Hilandarski razgovor,"* printed
in the literary review KNJIZEVNOST, (Belgrade 1984), p.327.

2. Since the time of preparation of this manuscript four novices have joined the
ranks of the monks.

Chilandar's Roster as of February 12, 1987:

Pro-Hegumen Nikanor Savic, b. 1903, Divci near Valjevo; in Chilandar since 1927.

Monk Pavle Lazovic, b. 1916, Luke near Dragachevo; in Chilandar since 1941.

Monk Simeon Andric, b. 1922, Stupnica near Loznica; in Chilandar since 1957.

Monk Arsenije Jovanovic, b. 1921, Milichnica near Valjevo; in Chilandar since 1957.

Monk Mitrofan Mishunic, b. 1923, Ratari near Smed. Palanka; in Chilandar since 1961. Editor of *Hilandar*.

Monk Damaskin Glavonic, b. 1902, Vincha near Kraljevo; in Chilandar since 1963.

Hieromonk Mojsije Zarkovic, b. 1923, Valjevska Kamenica; in Chilandar since 1964.

Hieromonk Hrisostom Stolic, b. 1939, Ruma-Srem; in Chilandar since 1969. Librarian.

Monk Mihailo Bogosavljevic, b. 1934, Sharanovo near Racha Kragujevachka; in Chilandar since 1970.

Monk Sava Lukic, b. 1908, Priboj-Bosna; in Chilandar since 1971.

Hieromonk Stefan Brankovic, b. 1950, Bozevac near Pozarevac; in Chilandar since 1974.

Monk Vasilije Urosevic, b. 1949, Brdjani near Gornji Milanovac; in Chilandar since 1975.

Hierodeacon Pajsije Tanasijevic, b. 1957, Chichevci-Bosnia; in Chilandar since 1978. Accomplished musician and connoisseur of medieval music.

Monk Serafim Spika, b. 1957, Belgrade; in Chilandar since 1981. Now in the House of Silence, Karyes.

Monk Pantelejmon Rat, b. 1947, Alpirsbach-Germany; in Chilandar since 1984. Working on German-Old Slavonic Liturgy and Prayer Book.

SELECTED BIBLIOGRAPHY

Akti Ruskago na Svjatom Afone monastira sv. velikomucenika i cjelitelja Panteleimona, Kiev, 1843

Archives de l'Athos, Fondee par Gabriel Millet, publiees par Paul Lamerle, Paris (continual series)

Atanasijevic, Dragutin. *Prvobitni-postanak imena i manastira Hilandara*, Beograd-Zemun, 1927

_____*Srpski arhiv Lavre Atonske*, "Spomenik" 56, SKA, Beograd, 1922

_____*SvetaGora u proslosti i sadasnjosti*, Srpski Knjizevni Glasnik 18, Beograd, 1907

Avramovic, Dimitrije. *Opisanie drevnosti srbski u svetoi (Atonskoi) gori s XIII litografisani tablica*, Beograd 1847

Barski, Vasilije Grigorovich. *Vtoroe posjescenie Svjatoi Afonskoi Gori*, St. Petersburg 1887

Basic, M.. *Stare srpske biografije*, Beograd 1924

Iz stare srpske knjizevnosti, Beograd 1926

Bogdanovic Dimitrije, Djuric J. Vojislav, Medakovic Dejan. *Hilandar*, Beograd 1978

Bogdanovic, D.. *Katalog cirilskih rukopisa manastira Hilandara*, Beograd 1978

_____*Izmirenje srpske i vizantijske crkve*, Naucni skup o Knezu Lazaru (papers), pp 81-91, Beograd 1975

Boskov, Vanco. *Mara Brankovic u turskim dokumentima iz Svete Gore*, Hilandarski zbornik 5, Beograd 1983

_____*Jedno originalno pismo-naredba (biti) Murata II za Svetu Goru*, Hilandarski zbornik 4, Beograd

Boskovic, Dj.. *Svetogoraki pabirci*, "Starinar" III, 1939

Burkovic, Tomo. *Hilandar u doba Nemanjica*, Beograd 1925

Byron, Robert. *The Station, Athos: Treasures and men*, London, 1949

Cavarnos, Constantine. *The Holy Mountain*, Belmont, Mass. 1973

Christou, Panagiotos. *To Hagion Oros: Historia, Menameja, Zoe*, Thessaloniki, 1970

Curzon, Robert. *Visits to Monasteries in the Levant* (eight editions 1849 -1916)

Cirkovic, Sima. *Srednjevekovna srpska drzava*, Zagreb 1959

Corovic, Vladimir. *Sveta Gora i Hilandar*, Beograd 1985

Cuk, Ruza. *Carica Mara*, Istoriski casopis, Beograd 1978

Danicic, Djuro. *Zivoti kraljeva i arhiepiskopa srpskih napisao Danilo i drugi*, Zagreb 1866

_____*Zivot Svetoga Save*, Beograd 1860

Dawkins, R. M.. *The Monks of Athos*, London 1936

Deroko, Aleksandar. *Mount Athos*, Belgrade 1967

Djuric, I.. *Pomenik Svetogorskog Protata s kraja XIV veka*, Zbornik Radova Vizantijskog Instituta 20, Beograd 1981

Djuric, V. J.. *Freske crkvice Sv. Besrebrenika despota Jovana Ugljese u Vatopedu*, ZRVI 7, Beograd 1961

Dolger, Franz. *Hagion Oros oder der Heilige Berg Athos*, Wien 1940

_____*Monchsland Athos*, München 1943

Ducic, Nicifor. *Starine Hilandarske*, Glasnik Srpskog Ucenog Drustva, Beograd 1884

Dujcev, I.. *Chilandar et Zographou au Moyen age*, Hilandarski zbornik I, 1966

Ferjancic, Bozidar. *Sava i katolici*, Istorija srpskog naroda II, Beograd 1984

Grassi, Emanuele. *Monte Athos*, Milano 1981

Grigorovic, V. I.. *Ocerk putesestvija po evropskoi Turcii*, Moskva 1877

Grivec, Franz. *Sveti Sava i Rim*, Ljubljana 1938

Grujic, Radoslav. *Carica Jelena i celija Sv. Save u Kareji*, Glasnik Skopskog naucnog drustva XIV, Skoplje 1935

_____*Gusari u Svetoj Gori i hilandarski pirg Hrusija*, Glasnik Skopskog naucnog drustva XIV, Skoplje 1935

Svetogorski azili za srpske vladaoce i vlastelu posle Kosovske bitke, Glasnik Skopskog ucenog drustva XI, Skoplje 1932

Hasluck, F. W.. *Athos and its Monasteries*, London 1924

Jagic, V.. *Tipik hilandarski i grcki izvor*, Spomenik SAN, XXXIV, Beograd 1898

Kasanin, Milan. *Srpska knjizevnost u srednjem veku*, Beograd 1975

Kasic, Dusan. *Manastir Hilandar i njegov znacaj u srpskoj istoriji* (from the Millenium volume: *Sveta Gora i manastir Hilandar, Beograd 1961*). *See other contributors as well.*

Kondakov, Nikodim Pavlovic. *Ikon Sinaskoi i Afonskoi kolekcii*, St. Petersburg 1902

―――*Pamjatniki Hristijanskago Iskustva na Afone*, St. Petersburg 1902

Lamerle, Paul. *Actes de Kutlumus* (Archives de l'Athos, No.2) Paris 1945-6

―――*Actes de Lavra* (Archives de l' Athos, No. 11, Paris 1982

Laskaris, Michail. *Actes Serbes de Vatopedi* ("Byzantinoslavica"VI), Praha 1936

Lefort, Jacques. *Actes d'Esphigmenou*, Paris 1973

Leonid (arhimandrit). *Istoriceskoe opisanije Serbskoi carskoi lavri Hilandara*, Moskva 1867

Loch, Sidney. *The Holy Mountain*, London 1957

Matejic, Mateja. *Manuscripts from the Chilandar Monastery, Mount Athos*. (Checklist of Slavic manuscripts), Columbus, Ohio, 1971/72

―――*Hilandar Slavic Codices*, Columbus, Ohio, 1976

―――*Hilandar Slavic Manuscripts*, Columbus, Ohio, 1972

―――*The Holy Mount and the Hilandar Monastery*, Columbus, Ohio,1983

(with Dragan Milivojevic). *An Antology of Medieval Serbian Literature in English*, Columbus, Ohio, 1978

Medakovic, Dejan. *Manastir Hilandar u XVIII veku*, Hilandarski zbornik 3, Beograd 1974

Mendieta, Emmanuel Amand de. *Mount Athos, The Garden of Panaghia*, Berlin 1972

Mirkovic, Lazar . *Hilandarski tipik Sv. Save* , Beograd 1935

―――*Zivoti Sv. Save i Stevana Prvovencanog*, Beograd 1938

Mosin, Vladimir. *Akti iz svetogorskih arhiva*,"Spomenik" SKA 91 , Beograd 1939

―――*Povelja kralja Milutina Karejskoj celiji,1318*, Glasnik Skopskog naucnog drustva XIX, - Skoplje 1938

―――*Svetogorski Protat* (reprint from"Starine", Vol. 43, Zagreb 1950

Mosin, V. - Purkovic, M.. *Hilandarski igumani Srednjeg veka*, Skoplje 1940

Mylonas, Paul M. . *Athos and Its Monasteries Through Old Engravings and Other Works of Art*, Millenium issue, Athens 1963

Nenadovic, S.. *Arhitektura Hilandara, crkve i paraklisi*, Hilandarski Zbornik 3, Beograd 1974

―――*Hilandar po grafickim prikazima XVIII i XIX stoleca, Zbornik Zastite spomenika kulture, XVI*, Beograd 1965

Nikolai, Bishop Velimirovic. *The Life of St. Sava*, Libertyville,Ill., 1951
John Julius Norwich and Reresby Sitwell with photographs by the
authors and A. Costa, *ATHOS*, New York 1966.
Novakovic, Stojan. *Istorija srpske knjizevnosti*, Beograd 1867
Oikonomides, Nicolas. *Actes de Dionisiou* , Paris 1978
_____*Actes de Kastamnonitou* , Paris 1978
Ostrogorski, Georg. *Serska oblast posle Dusanove smrti*, ZRVI, Beograd
1965
Parachrysanthou , Denise. *Actes de Protaton* , Paris 1975
Petkovic, Vladimir. *Legenda Svetog Save u starom zivopisu srpskom,
Glas SAN,CLIX*, Beograd 1933
Petrovic, Miodrag. *Povelja-pismo despota Jovana Ugljese iz 1368 g. o
izmirenju scrpske i carigradske crkve*, Istorijski casopis XXV-XXVI,
Beograd 1978 - 79
Purkovic, Miodrag. *Avinjonske pape i srpske zemlje*, Pozarevac 1934
_____*Srpski episkopi i mitropoliti Srednjeg veka*, "Hriscansko delo",
Skoplje 1937
Srpski patrijarsi Srednjeg veka, Glasnik Skopskog ucenog drustva 15 -
16, Skoplje 1936
Radojcic, Svetozar. *Umetnicki spomenici manastira Hilandara*, ZRVI ,
Beograd 1955
Radojicic, Djordje Sp.. *Stare srpske povelje i rukopisne knjige u Hilan-
daru* , Arhivist II, Beograd 1952
_____*Razvojni luk stare srpske knjizevnosti*, Novi Sad 1962
_____*Tvorci i dela stare srpske knjizevnosti*, Beograd 1963
Riley, Athelstan.*Athos or the mountain of the Monks*, London 1887
Sava Hilandarac. *Istorija i opis manastira Hilandara*, Beograd 1894
_____*Sveta Gora* , Beograd 1898
_____*Sava Nemanjic*, Zbirka "Istorija i Predanje" , SAN, Beograd
1976
Sherrard, Philipe. *Athos, The Holy Mountain*, London 1982
Simonopetritis, Andrew. *Holy Mountain, Bullwork of Orthodoxy and of
the Greek Nation* , Salonica 1969
Slijepcevic, Djoko. *Hilandarsko pitanje u XIX i pocetku XX veka*, Koln
1979
_____*Istorija srpske pravoslavne crkve*, Dusseldorf 1978
Smirnakes, Gerasimos. *To Agion Oros*, Athens 1903
Soulis, George Christos. *Tsar Stephen Düshan and Mount Athos*, Har-
vard Slavic Studies 2, 1954
_____*The Serbs and Byzantium during the reign of Tsar Stephen Dusan
(1331-1355) and his successors*, Washington D.C. 1966

Stanojevich, Milivoj S..*Early Yugoslav Literature*, Vol. I., New York 1922

Stanojevic, St. *Istorija srpskog naroda u Srednjem veku, Vol. I, O izvorima*, Beograd 1937

————*Sveti Sava i nezavisnost srpske crkve*, Beograd 1934

————*Studije o srpskoj diplomatici*, Glas SKA, Beograd 1928

Stewart, Cecile. *Byzantine Legacy* , London 1947

Tachiaos, A.E.. *Le monachisme Serbe de Saint Sava et la tradition hesychaste athonite*, Hilandarski zbornik I, Beograd 1966

————*Uloga Sv. Save u okviru slovenske knjizevne delatnosti na Svetoj Gori* (Istorija i Predanje), Beograd 1976

————*The Slavonic Manuscripts of St. Panteleimon Monastery (Rossikon) on Mount Athos*, Thessaloniki, Los Angeles 1981

Tatic, Zarko. *Tragom velike proslosti* , Beograd 1929

————*Sihasterija (posnica) Sv. Save u Kareji* , Glasnik Skopskog naucnog drustva, Skoplje 1930

Trifunovic, Djordje. *Primeri iz stare srpske knjizevnosti*, Beograd 1967

Uspenski, Porfirii. *Pervoe putesestvie v afonskie monastiri i skiti 1846 g.*, Kiev 1877

————*Vtoroe putesestvie po Svatoi Gore Afonskoi*, Moskva 1880

————*Visnjii Pokrov nad Afonom , Skazania* (Thaumaturgical images of Mt. Athos), Moskva 1902

Zakitonos, D..*Sveta Gora kao zajednica pravoslavlja i teznje za osamostaljenjem*, Hilandarski zbornik 1 . Beograd 1966

Zondiakos, Nicolas. *Les Institutions de l' Athos*, Strasbourg 1938

Zivojinovic, Mirjana. *Manastir Hilandari i Mileje*, Hilandarski zbornik 4, Beograd

————*Sveta Gora u doba Latinskog Carstva*,ZRVI XVII, Beograd 1976

————*Pirgovi svetogorskih manastira*, Beograd 1972

————*Svetogorci i stonski dohodak* , ZRVI XXII, Beograd 1983

A. CHRONOLOGY

330 A.D.	- Roman Emperor Constantine I builds the new capital (Constantinople)
843	- first historical mention of the Holy Mountain
883	- Emperor Basil I proclaims the autonomous status of the Holy Mountain
963	- Athanasios builds the Great Lavra
972	- Emperor John Tsimisces issues the first typikon of the Holy Mountain, generally known as Tragos.
1191	- Sava is shorn in Roussikon
1196	- Nemanya becomes monk Simeon in Studenitsa
1198	- Nemanya arrives on Mount Athos, meats Sava in Vatopediou.
1199	- Nemanya issues the *Founding Charter of Chilandar Monastery*
	- Sava establishes his hermitage in Karyes, writes its *Typikon* Nemanya dies
1206	- Sava transports the remains of Nemanya to Studenitsa
1208	- Sava writes *The Life of St. Simeon*
1219	- Sava obtains limited autocephaly for Serbian Church; becomes first archbishop.
c.1220	- Stephan the First-Crowned and Sava build Zhicha Monastery, the See of Serbia's Archbishopric.
1253	- the See of Serbia's Archbishopric is moved to Pech
c.1265	- Domentian and Theodosije co-author the biography of St. Sava
c.1303	- King Milutin replaces Nemanya's original church in Chilandar with a new building

1313-16	- Milutin issues *The Founding Charter* of Hrusija Pyrgos
1318	- Milutin issues *The Charter of Karyes Kellion*
1346	- Archbishopric of Serbia elevated to the Patriarchate by Tsar Dushan
1346-7	- Tsar Dushan (with family) visits the Holy Mountain
1355	- Dushan dies
1371	- Turks defeat Serbs at Maritsa River
c.1380	- Prince Lazar attaches his church to Chilandar's katholikon.
1387	- first incursions of Turkish units into the territory of Mount Athos take place
1389	- Prince Lazar perishes at Kosovo
1396	- First Crusade defeated at Nicopolis
1430	- Turkish occupation of Mount Athos
1453	- Fall of Constantinople
1459	- Fall of Smederevo. Serbia becomes Turkish Pashalic
1463	- the Patriarchate of Serbia abolished
1499	- Zeta falls under Turkish rule
1550	- Chilandarians venture to Moscow
1557	- Pech Patriarchate re-established.
1620	- George Mitrofanovic, Serbian iconographer, works in Chilandar.
1660	- Nikanor, former Venetian merchant, saves Chilandar from bankruptsy
1688	- Leopold I permits alms collecting in Austria to Chilandarians.
1772	- major blaze damages Chilandar
1766	- Pech Patriarchate abolished
1821	- Greek Uprising against Turks
1835	- Milosh Obrenovich helps Mount Athos monasteries
1846	- Dimitrije Avramovich records Serbian antiquities in Mount Athos monasteries.
1867	- Arcimandri. Leonid publishes in Moscoa a detailed description of Chilandar
1883	- Serbian Metropolitan Mihailo visits Chilandar
1884	- Archimandrite Nikifor Duchich reports on his visit to Chilandar
1894	- Monk Sava Chilandarats publishes his first book on Chilandar
1896	- King Aleksandar Obrenovich bails out Chilandar

1897	- First Comprehensive catalogue of Chilandar manuscripts published
1906	- revised and completed Catalogue of Chilandar books submitted to the Serbian Academy.
1925	- a team of professors and students of Belgrade and Skoplje universities visit Chilandar.
1930	- historian Vladimir Corovic works in Chilandar
1952-53	- teams of Serbian Academy members conduct extensive research projects in Chilandar
1963	- Holy Mountain Millenium is celebrated in Karyes
1966	- Byzantologist Georgij Ostrogorsky forms the Chilandar Committee of the Serbian Academy of Sciences and Arts in Belgrade.

B.   GLOSSARY OF ATHONITE TERMS

A

akathist - hymn honoring a saint, praising Christ, etc.
anchorite - one who renounces the world for religious reasons.
antiphony - two choirs in Greek churches singing alternatively.
apse - semicircular niche over the altar at the eastern end of Orthodox churches (also known as concha or apsida).
anchortarikion - monastery guest quarters.
arsana - monastery warf, usually comprising boat house, utility building, chapel for the caretaker and defense pyrgos.
athonite - pertaining to Athos.

B

bashta - monastery confessor.
basilica - rectangular or oblong building with a semicircular apse at the eastern end.

C

canon - rule formulated by the Holy Sinod; hymn (kanon)
cyrillic - Slavic alphabet adapted from Glagolic, named after St. Cyril.

D

domestikos - leading chanter of the choir
docheiar - monastery steward
docheion - storeroom for food, oil press, etc.

E

ecclesiarch -   superintendent of the main church, in charge of sacred
                  vessels, relics, etc. in the sanctuary
Eastern   community of Christian Churches that rejects the juris-
Orthodoxy -   diction of the Bishop of Rome
engage -   small boat
Evangelion -   four Gospel Books, with texts arranged to correspond
                  with liturgical cycle

F

fandarik -   reception room
fresco -   wall painting on wet mortar

G

gerontes -   elders in the monastery ("starats,")
gramata -   Russian charter (bull)

H

Hagaren -   Ismailite, infidel
Haghion Oros -   Holy Mountain
Hagiorite -   monk of the Holy Mountain (Svetogorats)
horologion -   liturgy book for holy days of the year
hossios -   holy, sacred
hieromonk -   monk authorized to conduct church services

I

icon -   a holy picture
iconostasis -   icon covered partition (altar screen) which separates the
                  nave from the sanctuary
illuminated   ornamented script, miniatures with fancy initial letters
manuscript -
inscribed cross - cruciform architectural design of the church plan

K

kaliva -   crude building or makeshift shelter dwelled by a solitary
                  monk
kathisma -   monk's dwelling place; also, section of the Psalter
katholikon -   main church in the monastery
kellion -   living unit in the monastery or dwelling outside of the
                  monastery

kontakion -   abbreviated hymn

ktytor -   donor, sponsor, founder of the monastery
kyr -   a Greek form of address for a man; master, Mister

L

Lavra -   highest ranking church; colony of monks
litiya -   prayer in the narthex or outdoor

M

Menaion -   one of the twelve books of hymns for each day of each
                   month
metoch -   monastery estate
monach -   monk

N

naos -   nave
narthex -   church vestibule preceding nave (eso-narthex) or facade
                   (exo-narthex)
nomokanon -   rules and regulations concerning the order in the church

P

portar -   gatekeeper; shuts door at sunset, opens at sunrise.
paracclesion -   side chapel or small church; Chilandar has 11 chapels.
Panaghia -   icon of Mother of God, or medal
Pantocrator -   the Omnipotent, (Jesus Christ, the Lord of the Universe)
parastos -   memorial service
Phiale -   baptismal font
Protos -   the highest monastic authority on the Holy Mountain,
                   the first among the equals

R

rasson -   monk's robe extending to ankles, with wide sleeves; it
                   gave name to Rassofore, the first grade (Little Habit)
                   among the monks, usually obtained after 3 years in the
                   monastery with the status of the novice.

S

semandron   wooden plank that serves in place of a bell or gong
(semantirion) -

schema -	monastic rank, based on three vows taken by monks to celibacy, poverty and obedience (called "lower schema" or "little schema"). Monks choosing to practice asceticism are ranked as "higher schema" (megaloschemos)

T

timpanum -	recess above the doorway, often with historic inscription
Theotokos -	Mother of God
trapeza -	refectory, decorated, with rows of wood or marble tables
triconch -	church with trefoil (clover) ground plan
troparion -	hymn sang as part of special services or on special days
typikon -	Rule, statute

Z

zograph -	itinerant mural or icon painter

PERSONAL NAMES

A

Aleksei Mihailovich, Russian tsar, 16
Alexios III Angelos, Byzantine
emperor, 1 ,36, 38, 104, 113, 133
Ananios, patriarch, 17
Anastasia, tsarina, 96
Andreas, Hungarian king, 49
Andronikos II Palaeologos, emperor,
17, 25, 62, 63, 64, 65
Angelina, despotess, 95-96
Anne, Serbian queen, 19
Antonii, of Kiev, 18
Antonije, of Banja, 101
Antonije, Bagash, Pagases, 18, 94
Aristotle, 5
Arsenije, archbishop, 56
Arsenije, Chil. delegate, 95
Arsenije, Chil. confessor, 31
Arsenije, pro-hegumen, 72, 73
Arsenije, alms collector, 100
Arsenije, protos, 134
Arsenije, Chil. elder, 108
Arsenije, librarian, 126
Arsenije Charnojevic, patriarch, 129
Atanasije, Chil. scribe, 87
Athanasios, St., of Lavra, 6, 10, 112
Athanasios, of Jerusalem, 63
Averkije, Karyes scribe, 88
Avil, mercenary, 135
Avramovic, Dimitrije, artist, 19, 109-
10

B

Barski, Vasili Grigorovich, author, 114
Beckovic, Matija, poet, 136
Billington, James H., author, 71
Bogdanovic, Mitrofan, Chilandarian
from Dalmatia, 101
Brankovic, Djuradj, despot, 18, 20, 94
Mara, sultaness, 18, 95, 96
Stefan, despot, 95
Vuk, grandee, 93

C

Catheline, Serb. queen, 85
Catherine the Great, tsarina, 17
Charles d'Anjou, king, 59
Chelandarios, athonite, 38
Cherny,Vadim (Charnojevic), 129
Clement III, pope, 52
Clement V, pope, 61
Chrysostom, librarian, 126
Chrysostom, protos 134
Constantine, king of Greece, 122
Constantine, Russian grand duke, 112
Corovic, Vladimir, historian, 72
Cvijetko, of Vidin, 111
Cyril, of St. Paul's, 95

D

Damaskinos, St., (see John Damascene)
Damian, Chil. scribe, 87

GEOGRAPHICAL NAMES

A

Adrianopolis, city in Thrace, 74

Aegean Sea, 5

St. Andrew's, Russian skete, 112

Antivari (today's Bar), 51, 52, 57

Arcadia, ancient region on Peloponnesos (Greece), 25

Athos, mountain peak, 10, 72

Austria, historic (former empire in Central Europe), 98

"Axion Estin," Karyes icon, 26

B

Bar (see Antivari)

Banja (monastery, Gulf of Kotor), 101

Banjska, monastery in Serbia, 65, 86

St. Basil's, chapel at Hrusija ("Pyrgos at the Sea"), 84

Belgrade, 116, 118

Berlin, Congress of, 116

Boka Kotorska (Gulf of Kotor), 101

Brnjatsi (queen's palace), 65

Byzantium, successor state of Roman Empire, 1, 49, 52

C

Chalcidice (Khalkidiki), peninsula, 5, 64

Chelantarion (ancient site of Chilandar), 16, 38, 39

Chilandar - churches and chapels, 29, 111, 125

- hospital, 43

- konakia, 32, 33

- library, 124-26

- "houses", 96, 99, 115

- metochia 97, 118

- pyrgoi (towers) 82, 84

Cologne, 45

Constantinople, 10, 38, 41, 52, 73, 93, 109

Cyprus, 11

D

Dalmatia, historic, 101, 103

Daphne, port of entry, 25

Dechani, monastery in Serbia, 89

St. Dimitrije's, church (Pech Patriarchate), 63

Dimotika, 74

Dion, pagan port, 11

Dionisiou, Athos monastery, 16, 20, 22

Docheiariou, Athos monastery, 17, 20, 22

Dubrovnik, historic, 57, 61, 95

E

St. Elias, Russian skete, 17

Epirus, Despotate of, 50

1. *Courtyard of Chilandar Monastery. The tall cyprus trees, the baptismal
    font wedged in between, the katholikon in the background—make an
    indelible impression on incoming visitors.*

2. *Of the five wonder-making icons in Chilandar, the Three-Handed Virgin Mary is the most venerated by the monks.*

3. The icon of the Virgin nursing Christ. It was brought by St. Sava from Jerusalem, 1229-30.

4. The Pro-Hegumen of Chilander Monastery, Father Nikanor.

5. *The youngest Protos in the history of the Holy Mountain, Hierodeacon Pajsije of Chilandar.*

6. *Lead-plated roofs of Chilandar's katholicon provide an intricate pattern, as seen from St. Sava Tower.*

(Courtesy Dr. G. Nikolich)

7. *St. Sava Tower, bulwark of Chilandar's defense system. The Chapel of the Holy Archangels is seen at bottom, and the recently-built new Library Building is on the right.*

(Courtesy Dr. G. Nikolich)

8. *Monk Simeon, custodian of St. Sava's Hermitage in Karyes "House of Silence".*

9. *Cave-like cubicle where St. Sava spent days and nights in prayer,
prostrations and meditations, practicing the strictest form of
aestheticism, is part of Sava's Hermitage in Karyes.*

10. *Monk Mitrofan of Chilandar bidding farewell to author at the small
"arsana" (port) of the monastery.*
(Courtesy A. Gaon)